300
Papermaking
Recipes

Mary Reimer & Heidi Reimer-Epp

Martingale ®
& C O M P A N Y

A Quarto Book

Martingale®
& COMPANY

First published in 2000 by Martingale & Company
20205 144th Ave, NE, Woodinville, WA 98072-8478
www.martingale-pub.com

Library of Congress Cataloging-in-Publication data available.

ISBN 1-56477-533-X

QUAR PPTT

Conceived, designed, and produced by Quarto Publishing plc
The Old Brewery
6 Blundell Street
London
N7 9BH

Editor Kate Michell
Art Editor Sally Bond
Assistant Art Director Penny Cobb
Text Editors Claire Waite, Sam Merrel, Geoff Barker
Designer Julie Francis
Photographer Colin Bowling
Indexer Dorothy Frame

Art Director Moira Clinch
Publisher Piers Spence

Manufactured in China by Regent Publishing Services, Ltd
Printed in China by SNP Leefung Printers Ltd

07 06 05 04   6 5 4 3 2

Safety Notice
Papermaking can be dangerous, and readers should follow safety procedures and wear protective goggles at all times during the preparation of chemicals and cooking of alkaline pulp mixtures. Neither the author, copyright holders, nor publishers of this book can accept legal liability for any damage or injury sustained as a result of papermaking.

Contents

Introduction

What makes this book different from all the other books on hand papermaking? Chances are that you are one of the many people who were drawn into the world of hand papermaking after reading an attractive and informative book on the subject. We are unable to resist a new book on papermaking, especially if it contains something novel that will inspire us and stretch the boundaries of our knowledge and experience. It is wonderful to experiment, to try new approaches and new products, but there are certain techniques and combinations which provide an essential base of papermaking knowledge from which you can develop your own ideas and move ahead. This book, *300 Papermaking Recipes*, provides that base by showing the results of and giving the recipes and instructions for 300 different paper types. By combining, changing, and adding to various pulp types, we have been able to produce this comprehensive guide which will save hours of research, freeing papermakers to follow their own creative paths. This is a book to read, to look at, and to enjoy. Most of all, however, it is a practical guide, a reference aid, and, we believe, an important tool for hand papermakers. Be inspired by the following gallery of paper art, only a few examples of what can be done with your handmade paper.

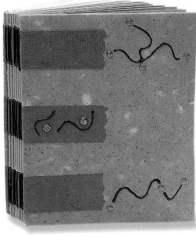

▼ **Pocket Journal**
Heidi Reimer-Epp

The cover of this Pocket Journal is made of tea paper whereas the inner jacket is recycled blue. The handsewn binding allows the book to be opened flat, which facilitates writing on both sides of the page. The strap binding is durable abaca paper.

▲ **'Molluscs'**
Stuart Bullen

Artist Stuart Bullen chose to use a sheet of plain handmade cotton paper as the canvas for a colorful mixed media print.

▶ Twig Weaving
Heidi Reimer-Epp

Torn strips of handmade paper are woven on a frame of twigs and tied with natural jute.

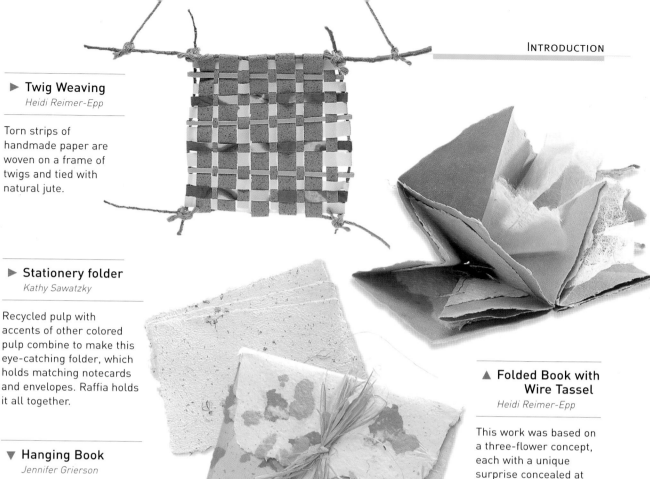

▶ Stationery folder
Kathy Sawatzky

Recycled pulp with accents of other colored pulp combine to make this eye-catching folder, which holds matching notecards and envelopes. Raffia holds it all together.

▲ Folded Book with Wire Tassel
Heidi Reimer-Epp

This work was based on a three-flower concept, each with a unique surprise concealed at the center and revealed only when opened up.

▼ Hanging Book
Jennifer Grierson

An innovative outdoor installation, using a variety of handmade papers, brings the paper back to its natural origins.

◄ Blue Beach
Mary Reimer

Pigmented pulp was poured and fragments of glass were embedded in the wet pulp. A photo of a dog and of a woman's face were placed under two of the clear glass fragments. Then the piece was placed on a vacuum table to remove the water without damaging the pulp.

▲ Framed Lino Cut
Heidi Reimer-Epp

This book contains handmade pages of abaca and the cover paper is plain abaca with an overlay of petal paper. The book is bound by hand, using embroidery floss and a Stab binding. The cover had a small lino cut placed behind a frame.

► Threaded Square
Mary Reimer

A criss-cross pattern of threads laminated between two layers of flax were left to air dry. The flax shrinks but the threads restrain the shrinkage, so the resulting form is interesting in both shape and texture.

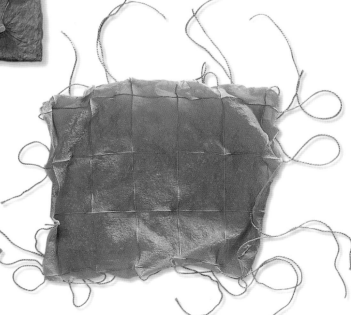

▲ Softy
Heidi Reimer-Epp

This soft cover book has cotton pages and a decorative pulp pull-away cover. The several layers of pulp give firmness and strength to the soft cover.

▼ Molded abaca bowl
Heidi Reimer-Epp

Formed from abaca and petal sheets and embellished with raffia and gold wire, this little bowl is a whimsical example of handmade paper art.

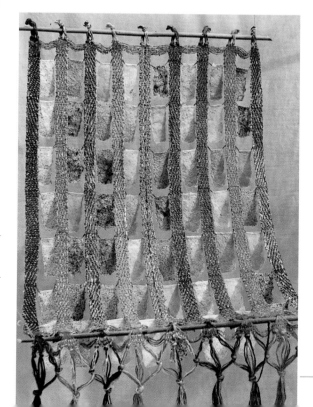

▲ Eastern Delights
Heidi Reimer-Epp

Cotton pages with crushed yellow petals make up this book. The cover is pigmented cotton with a mixed petal scattering. The Thai leaf is affixed to a square of sage abaca and the book is bound with white woven ribbon in Japanese Stab Binding.

▶ Forest Flags
Jennifer Grierson

A variety of handmade papers combined with handweaved fabric creates a warm, original wall hanging for your home.

7

Setting Up

The best thing about home papermaking is that it requires very little equipment to produce excellent results. Apart from a few essential items, most of the setup equipment is open to improvisation and can be easily assembled for use in the kitchen, garage, or yard. Non-waterproof surface areas can be protected using plastic sheets, and the papermaker would be wise to wear rubber boots and a rubber apron.

One of the most important pieces of papermaking equipment is the mold and deckle. A well-made mold and deckle set will save the frustration of constant repair and replacement of poorly designed and constructed models. The mold is the screen-covered frame upon which the sheet of paper is formed. The deckle is a frame that is placed on the mold to define the edge of the paper. If you are making your own molds and deckles, picture frames with screening stretched across and glued or stapled are suitable, and use brass fittings, waterproof glue, and several coats of liquid plastic coating.

Purchased molds and deckles often have a screen of heat-shrinking polypropylene which keeps its shape better than regular screening and can be tightened in the event of sagging by a few passes of a hot blow-dryer. Picture frames, embroidery hoops, and spatter screens for the frying pan all make adequate temporary molds and deckles.

A 5 x 7-inch (125 x 175-mm) mold and deckle can be used in an average-sized washbowl, while an 8½ x 11-inch (215 x 280-mm) one works best in a slightly larger vat. Design a system which works best for you.

A kitchen blender is useful for blending semi-processed and recycled pulp. When cooking with the alkaline solution used to break down fibrous plant material, a non-enameled cooking pot is best.

The most convenient and cost-effective pressing system is a set of boards and two sets of C-clamps which will press and stack several sheets at a time, and will remove sufficient water to allow for hanging up to air dry. Be sure to use several coats of polyurethane to waterproof the boards and preserve their usefulness.

▲ Assembled papermaking equipment

The basic papermaking tools include a blender, a stack of kitchen towels or pieces of cotton sheets, a plastic washbowl, and a mold and deckle. A wire whisk is helpful to keep the pulp particles in the water evenly dispersed.

▲ Mold and deckle making

Beyond the traditional papermaker's mold-and-deckle set, try using a variety of shapes and screening, such as a pantyhose stretched over a coat hanger.

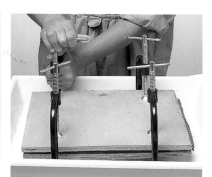

▲ Three basic pulp types

Paper can be made from an endless variety of pulp types. Semi-processed pulp is available in several forms from papermaking suppliers. Cotton and abaca pulps are readily available for a reasonable price, and make long-lasting, beautiful sheets. Recycled office paper, brown paper bags, and many common field and garden plants may be prepared as pulp for papermaking.

Pulp preparation

Semi-processed pulp or sheets of used office paper can be torn into pieces about 1 inch square (25mm), soaked overnight, or for at least 1 hour. Process a few pieces at a time in a blender three-quarters full of water until smooth, then strain the pulp for 2 minutes. Four cups of pulp will make about 20 sheets of 5 x 7-inch (125 x 175-mm) paper.

Pressing equipment

Press layers of couched sheets and interfacing material between two waterproofed boards. Secure with C-clamps and gradually increase the pressure as the water is released from the stack. When no more water is running out, continue to press for about 10 minutes.

Getting to Work!

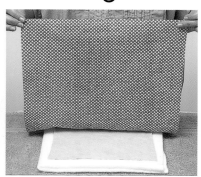

TIP Removing the deckle

Preparing a couching area

Prepare either a pad of newspaper, blankets, or towels as a bed for your stack. Place a sheet of kitchen cloth or sheeting on top of the pad. As each sheet is formed, cover it with two sheets of material before couching the next sheet.

Pulling a sheet

Fill the washbowl with eight cups (2 liters) of water. Add two cups of prepared pulp and whisk to distribute the pulp evenly. Holding the mold and deckle (be sure that the mold is screen-side up!) by the shorter sides, position it below the surface of the pulp, lift it out of the washbowl, and allow the water to drain.

Remove the deckle from the mold with care so as to avoid dripping on the freshly formed sheet. The thickness of a sheet is determined by the proportion of pulp to water; you will have to experiment with ratios to achieve your desired effect.

Couching and forming a post

Using the prepared couching surface (see page 9), hold the mold in an upright position and rest the frame on the edge of the couching pad nearest you. In a smooth rolling motion, roll the sheet from the edge near you across the couching surface, releasing the sheet. A good mold and deckle makes this easier and the success rate improves with practice.

TIP Removing sticky sheets

If the paper sticks to the mold, try blotting the excess water with a sponge and loosening one corner. Cover the new sheet with two layers of couching material before couching the next sheet on top. A stack of sheets is called a post. When you have a post of 10 to 20 sheets, move the entire post to the pressing board.

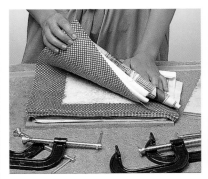

Pressing: stage one

Cover the top of the stack with a piece of wool blanket or thick towels before adding the second board (see page 9). Secure with C-clamps or place bricks or weights on top, increasing the pressure or weight as water runs out.

Pressing: stage two

The pressed sheet may be hung to dry on its couching sheet and then lightly ironed to smooth it out. If sizing (stiffening agent) has not been added to the pulp, a coating of spray starch may be added at this time.

TIP Smoothing with a roller

A pressed sheet may be transferred to a smooth glass, wood, or Plexiglas surface and smoothed with a roller. This will produce one very smooth side and a rougher side, the one which was not against the smooth surface.

Drying

Construct a simple dryer stack using layers of waterproofed plywood, corrugated cardboard, thick paper, the sheet of pressed damp paper, followed by thick paper, cardboard, and plywood again. Stack these "sandwiches" together, and place weights, such as bricks, on top of the stack. Position an electric fan to blow air away from the dryer to pull damp air out of the dryer and draw dry air in on the opposite side.

Texture and Technique

By using some basic techniques and materials, the papermaker may add unique textural qualities and dimension to a sheet of paper. Couching onto textured surfaces produces paper with interesting form and detail. Adding plants, threads, bits of fabric all add personality to the product. Painting, pouring, and layering with colored pulp, and adding inclusions such as glass are possibilities with which to experiment.

Textured surface assortment

Couch paper on a variety of surfaces in order to achieve unique textural results. Baskets, bowls, ceiling grids, bamboo mats, netting, tulle, and lace are fun to experiment with. Toweling produces paper with a surface appreciated by many artists.

Embedding and laminating

Build up layers by laminating layers of pulp, using plants, string, dried fruit, and colored pulp between the sheets. Remove sections of a base sheet and laminate one of a different color on top to expose layers of color and shape in the final piece.

Embossing

For the clearest imprint, couch the paper directly onto the object or surface and allow it to dry in position. Leaves, string, lace, and cardboard are all useful embossing tools. When the paper has dried, carefully remove the embossed article.

Pulp painting

Make a base sheet of paper and use a turkey baster, syringes, or "squeeze" bottles filled with colored pulp to create designs or pictures. Over-beaten abaca pulp or other long fiber pulp is pigmented and diluted. Add formation aid to prevent the fibers from sticking together.

Pouring and embedding

Use a picture frame or deckle to restrain pulp which is poured into the shape and allowed to air dry. Or use cake pans and cookie molds to make shapes for collages and pictures, and embed small stones, pieces of colored glass, or seashells for a unique way to display your treasures.

Layering

Scratch away some of the base pulp before laminating a second sheet. Embed ribbon or string for an interesting effect. Combine colors, shapes, and pulp types in partial layers. When the paper is either wet or dry, pull the string to create dimension and texture.

11

Papermaking with Plant Fibers

Many papermakers believe that the ultimate experience in papermaking is the creation of paper from plant fibers. Locally grown plants are often wonderful sources of fiber, and with some patience, skill, and labor, a papermaker can achieve beautiful results. Work in a well-ventilated space and use a large, non-enameled cooking pot.

Most plants require chopping and cooking before being used as pulp. Some also require treatment with an alkaline solution to break down the cellulose into usable pulp and to separate the non-fibrous plant material which is discarded. Once the plant fiber has been broken down, it may be used alone or in combination with other pulp types, such as cotton, to make strong and beautiful paper.

A cost-efficient and often readily available alkaline solution is made by boiling firewood ash in a large pot of water. When the plant fiber is brought to a boil in the alkaline solution, it should then be simmered until the fiber can be pulled apart easily. This material should be placed in a colander or netting and rinsed with cold water until the rinse water runs clear.

Working with these plant pulps can be tricky, but the beauty and feel of the finished product makes it well worth the effort.

WARNING

- Any cooking of wood ash or plant materials must be done in a very well-ventilated area. Outside would be ideal.

- You should wear protective clothing—rubber apron, rubber boots, goggles to protect the eyes and gloves to avoid splashes to the skin.

Cooking with firewood ash

Fill the cooking pot to the halfway point with ashes. Add sufficient cold water to cover the ashes and continue pouring to raise the level to the three-quarters full point. Bring to a boil in a well-ventilated space, stirring to dissolve most of the ash. Strain several times and discard the wet ashes. Save the alkaline solution, avoiding any contact with the skin.

Cooking plant materials

Fill the cooking pot with plant material. Add the alkaline solution slowly and carefully. Stirring frequently, bring this solution to a boil and simmer for half an hour, or until the material has broken down.

Rinsing

Rinse several times in cold water to flush out the remaining alkaline solution. The plant material is ready to be blended into pulp as it is, or combined half-and-half with cotton or recycled pulp for added strength.

Blending plant pulp

Add half a cup of plant fiber to a blender three-quarters full of water. Blending for a few seconds will produce a coarse paper, while increased blending will refine the pulp and the paper will be smoother and contain fewer large flecks.

TIP Testing pulp consistency

To determine whether or not the fibers have been sufficiently broken down, take a pinch of plant material, put it into a jar of cold water, and shake the jar for one minute (don't forget to put the lid on!). If the fibers appear to be evenly distributed with no clumping, it is ready to be used as pulp and formed into sheets.

Couching plant fiber sheets

It may feel as though there is not much pulp on the mold when you couch your first sheet, but go ahead and couch it—you will be surprised at the way in which the fibers have interwoven to cover the screen.

Cotton and Abaca Pulps

One of the delights of papermaking is the wide variety of pulp sources available for producing wonderful paper types: recycled paper is often the first source for the home papermaker; vegetable pulp is interesting to produce and results in beautiful specialty papers; but for consistent quality and long-lasting paper, the use of semi-processed pulp is highly recommended. Cotton and unbleached abaca are the most readily available semi-processed pulp types (see the Resource Directory on page 94 for sources of semi-processed pulp).

The following pages look at the many ways in which you can use color and other materials to enhance both cotton and abaca pulps. Use the samples illustrated here to observe the different reactions of pulp types to fabric dye and other inclusions.

These recipes use pre-prepared pulp and show you how to add extra ingredients to make unique pulps ready for pulling, couching, pressing, and drying. For instructions on turning pulp into paper, see pages 8 to 13.

Cotton and Abaca Pulp Samplers

Cotton pulp produces a pure white sheet which is easily pigmented with fabric dye, or it can be colored with special pigments available from papermaking suppliers. Unbleached abaca fibers are longer than cotton and creamy beige in color. This pulp also accepts dye or pigments well and the sheets are strong and long-lasting.

1 Pure Cotton

- 1 CUP COTTON PULP

1 Prepare the cotton pulp according to the directions on pages 8 to 13.

2 Couch cotton sheets on very clean cloths, as white cotton pulp picks up any colorants remaining from previous projects. Makes a sheet of crisp white paper.

2 Pure Unbleached Abaca

- 1 CUP ABACA PULP

Prepare the abaca pulp according to the directions on pages 8 to 13. Makes a creamy, natural tan-colored paper.

3 Dotted Abaca

- 1 CUP ABACA PULP
- 2 TABLESPOONS (30ML) SMALL BLACK DOTS, PUNCHED FROM CONSTRUCTION PAPER
- 1 TABLESPOON (15ML) LARGE BROWN DOTS, PUNCHED FROM BROWN PAPER BAG

1 Pour the pulp into a bowl and mix in the paper dots with a spoon or with your hands. Ensure there is an even distribution of dots within the pulp.

2 Add the pulp to the vat of water and whisk well with a wire whisk. Makes a creamy abaca paper with large and small dots throughout.

4 Blue Metallic Speckled Cotton

- 1 CUP COTTON PULP
- ¼ CUP BLUE TINSEL, CUT INTO ½-INCH (13-MM) PIECES

1 Add the tinsel pieces to the cotton pulp by hand or with a spoon, and mix to achieve an even distribution of material.

2 Add the pulp to the vat filled with water and mix well by hand. Creates a white paper with elegant metallic blue lines.

Cotton Pulp Enhanced with Fabric Dye

Follow the manufacturer's instructions when diluting fabric dye with water. For full-strength color use the ratios suggested by the manufacturer, for lighter shades double the amount of water you mix with the dye.

Let the colored pulp sit overnight before pulling sheets, to allow for best color absorption. Store pulp that is being used over a period of days by draining the water and placing the pulp in a labeled, airtight container in the refrigerator.

5 Pink Cotton

- 1 CUP COTTON PULP
- 1 CUP (250ML) RED FABRIC DYE DILUTED TO HALF THE STRENGTH SPECIFIED BY THE MANUFACTURER

1 Pour the diluted fabric dye into a bucket with the cotton pulp.

2 Mix the pulp and dye together by hand until evenly blended to obtain a light pink paper.

7 Lemon Cotton

- 1 CUP COTTON PULP
- 1 CUP (250ML) YELLOW FABRIC DYE DILUTED TO HALF THE STRENGTH SPECIFIED BY THE MANUFACTURER

1 Pour the diluted fabric dye into a bucket with the cotton pulp.

2 Mix the pulp and dye together by hand until evenly mixed to obtain a light yellow paper.

6 Sky Blue Cotton

- 1 CUP COTTON PULP
- 1 CUP (250ML) BLUE FABRIC DYE DILUTED TO HALF THE STRENGTH SPECIFIED BY THE MANUFACTURER

1 Add the diluted fabric dye to the cotton pulp in a bucket.

2 Mix by hand until the pulp and dye are evenly blended to obtain a light blue paper.

8 Lime Cotton

- 1 CUP COTTON PULP
- 1 CUP (250ML) GREEN FABRIC DYE DILUTED TO HALF THE STRENGTH SPECIFIED BY THE MANUFACTURER

1 Add the mixed fabric dye to the cotton pulp in a bucket.

2 Mix by hand until the pulp and dye are evenly blended to obtain a light green paper.

9 Fiery Red Cotton

- 1 CUP COTTON PULP
- 1 CUP (250ML) RED FABRIC DYE MIXED TO THE FULL STRENGTH SPECIFIED BY THE MANUFACTURER

1 Add the prepared fabric dye to the cotton pulp in a bucket.

2 Mix by hand until evenly blended to make a deep scarlet paper.

11 Dark Yellow Cotton

- 1 CUP COTTON PULP
- 1 CUP (250ML) YELLOW FABRIC DYE MIXED TO THE FULL STRENGTH SPECIFIED BY THE MANUFACTURER

1 Add the prepared fabric dye to the cotton pulp in a bucket.

2 Mix by hand until the pulp and dye are evenly blended to produce a dark yellow paper.

10 Deep Blue Cotton

- 1 CUP COTTON PULP
- 1 CUP (250ML) BLUE FABRIC DYE MIXED TO THE FULL STRENGTH SPECIFIED BY THE MANUFACTURER

1 Pour the prepared fabric dye into a bucket with the cotton pulp.

2 Mix the pulp and dye together by hand until evenly blended to produce a deep blue paper.

12 Deep Green Cotton

- 1 CUP COTTON PULP
- 1 CUP (250ML) GREEN FABRIC DYE MIXED TO THE FULL STRENGTH SPECIFIED BY THE MANUFACTURER

1 Add the prepared fabric dye to the cotton pulp in a bucket.

2 Mix by hand until the pulp and dye are evenly blended to produce a deep green paper.

Abaca Pulp Enhanced with Fabric Dye

Coloring abaca pulp with fabric dye follows the same process as coloring cotton pulp, but the effects are quite different. Let the colored pulp sit overnight before pulling sheets, to allow for best color absorption.

Abaca pulp decomposes more quickly than cotton pulp so it is imperative that you store it by draining out the water and placing the pulp in a labeled, airtight container in the refrigerator.

14 Pastel Violet Abaca

- 1 CUP ABACA PULP
- 1 CUP (250ML) VIOLET FABRIC DYE DILUTED TO HALF THE STRENGTH SPECIFIED BY THE MANUFACTURER

1 Add the diluted fabric dye to the abaca pulp in a bucket.

2 Mix by hand until the pulp and dye are evenly blended to create a pale violet paper.

13 Pale Pink Abaca

- 1 CUP ABACA PULP
- 1 CUP (250ML) RED FABRIC DYE DILUTED TO HALF THE STRENGTH SPECIFIED BY THE MANUFACTURER

1 Pour the diluted fabric dye into a bucket with the abaca pulp.

2 Mix the pulp and dye together by hand until evenly blended to make a pale pink paper.

15 Peach Abaca

- 1 CUP ABACA PULP
- 1 CUP (250ML) ORANGE FABRIC DYE DILUTED TO HALF THE STRENGTH SPECIFIED BY THE MANUFACTURER

1 Pour the diluted fabric dye into a bucket with the abaca pulp.

2 Mix the pulp and dye together by hand until evenly blended to obtain a pale peach paper.

17

18

19

20

16 Tan Abaca

- 1 CUP ABACA PULP
- 1 CUP (250ML) BROWN FABRIC DYE DILUTED TO HALF THE STRENGTH SPECIFIED BY THE MANUFACTURER

1 Add the diluted fabric dye to the abaca pulp in a bucket.

2 Mix by hand until the pulp and dye are evenly blended to produce a pale tan paper.

18 Violet Abaca

- 1 CUP ABACA PULP
- 1 CUP (250ML) VIOLET FABRIC DYE MIXED TO THE FULL STRENGTH SPECIFIED BY THE MANUFACTURER

1 Add the prepared fabric dye to the abaca pulp in a bucket.

2 Mix the pulp and dye together by hand until evenly blended to create brilliant violet paper.

17 Fuchsia Abaca

- 1 CUP ABACA PULP
- 1 CUP (250ML) FUCHSIA FABRIC DYE MIXED TO THE FULL STRENGTH SPECIFIED BY THE MANUFACTURER

1 Pour the prepared fabric dye into a bucket with the abaca pulp.

2 Mix by hand until the pulp and dye are evenly blended to produce a deep fuchsia paper.

19 Tangerine Abaca

- 1 CUP ABACA PULP
- 1 CUP (250ML) ORANGE FABRIC DYE MIXED TO THE FULL STRENGTH SPECIFIED BY THE MANUFACTURER

1 Pour the prepared fabric dye into a bucket with the abaca pulp.

2 Mix by hand until the pulp and dye are evenly blended to produce a deep orange paper.

20 Chocolate Brown Abaca

- 1 CUP ABACA PULP
- 1 CUP (250ML) BROWN FABRIC DYE MIXED TO THE FULL STRENGTH SPECIFIED BY THE MANUFACTURER

1 Add the prepared fabric dye to the abaca pulp in a bucket.

2 Mix the pulp and dye together by hand until evenly blended to obtain a dark brown paper.

Dyed Pulp Medleys

Many of the recipes for dyed cotton and abaca pulps can be mixed together to create new colors and textures. You will no doubt notice that the abaca flecks form into long strands in the pulp while the cotton fibers produce heavier clumps. This is because the fibers of the cotton plant are much shorter than those of abaca. Try exploiting these qualities by mixing the two pulps together.

21

24

25

26

21 Purple Explosion Cotton Mix

- 1 CUP DEEP BLUE COTTON PULP
- ½ CUP FIERY RED COTTON PULP
- WATER

Place the pulps in the vat of water, and blend evenly with a wire whisk. Creates a mottled purple paper.

22 Stewed Pumpkins Medley

- 1 CUP TANGERINE ABACA PULP
- ½ CUP SKY BLUE COTTON PULP
- WATER

Put the colored pulps together in the vat with water and blend evenly with a wire whisk to produce a brownish pulp flecked with orange and blue.

23 Purple Passion Combination

- 1 CUP DEEP BLUE COTTON PULP
- ½ CUP FUCHSIA ABACA PULP
- WATER

Place the pulps in the vat with water and blend together evenly with a wire whisk. Paper will be purple with long flecks of fuchsia abaca pulp.

24 Green Curry Mix

- 1 CUP DEEP GREEN COTTON PULP
- ½ CUP TANGERINE ABA[CA] PULP
- WATER

Put the colored pulps in [the] vat with water and mix together evenly using a wire whisk. Creates an orange-green pulp with orange flecks.

22

23

27

28

25 Blue Lava Lamp Cotton Mix

- 1 CUP DARK YELLOW COTTON PULP
- $\frac{1}{2}$ CUP SKY BLUE COTTON PULP
- WATER

In the vat with water, use a wire whisk to blend the colored pulps to produce a beautiful yellow pulp accented with blue blobs.

26 Azure Sea Cotton Combination

- 1 CUP SKY BLUE COTTON PULP
- $\frac{1}{2}$ CUP LIME COTTON PULP
- WATER

Put the colored pulps in the vat with water and mix together evenly using a wire whisk. Colors will melt together to create a turquoise paper with green flecks.

27 Candy Orange Cotton Creation

- 1 CUP LEMON COTTON PULP
- $\frac{1}{2}$ CUP PINK COTTON PULP
- WATER

In the vat with water, use a wire whisk to blend the colored pulps. The pink pulp will deepen the yellow pulp to a light orange and add flecks of pink.

28 Purple Cotton Candy Abaca Mix

- 1 CUP PASTEL VIOLET ABACA PULP
- $\frac{1}{2}$ CUP VIOLET ABACA PULP
- WATER

Put the colored pulps in the vat with water and mix together evenly using a wire whisk. Makes a pale violet paper flecked with dark violet.

21

Confetti Inclusions

Homemade confetti can be easily produced using a hole punch which lets you make holes of varying sizes. This method allows for specific paper types to be prepared: try making confetti from foil wrapping paper, colorful paper napkins, and other interesting sources. The red apple and cupid shapes can be made using a specialty hole punch available from stationery and craft stores.

29 Brown Paper Bag Dots in Cotton

- 1 CUP COTTON PULP
- 2 TABLESPOONS (30ML) DOTS PUNCHED FROM BROWN PAPER BAG

Use your hands to gently mix the brown dots into the cotton pulp, evenly distributing the shapes. This recipe is a great way to reuse unwanted bags.

30 Red Apple Confetti in Cotton

- 1 CUP COTTON PULP
- 2 TABLESPOONS (30ML) APPLE CONFETTI PUNCHED FROM RED CONSTRUCTION PAPER

Use your hands to gently mix the red apple confetti into the cotton pulp until the material is evenly distributed. The white paper will be accented with red apple confetti.

31 White Cupids in Pink Cotton

- 1 CUP PINK COTTON PULP
- 2 TABLESPOONS (30ML) CUPID CONFETTI PUNCHED FROM WHITE BOND PAPER

Use your hands to gently mix the white cupid confetti into the colored cotton pulp until the shapes are evenly distributed. The white cupids will float in a sky of pink paper.

32 White Dots in Lemon Cotton

- 1 CUP LEMON COTTON PULP
- 2 TEASPOONS (10ML) SMALL DOTS PUNCHED FROM WHITE PAPER

Use your hands to gently mix the small white dots into the colored cotton pulp until the dots are evenly distributed. Lemon paper will be lightly accented with white dots.

22

35 Black Dotted Fiery Red Cotton

- 1 CUP FIERY RED COTTON PULP
- 1 TEASPOON (5ML) SMALL DOTS, CUT FROM BLACK PAPER

Use your hands to blend the black dots and colored pulp, evenly distributing the paper shapes. Red paper will be lightly accented with black dots.

36 Magazine Dots in Cotton

- 1 CUP COTTON PULP
- 2 TABLESPOONS (30ML) DOTS PUNCHED FROM MAGAZINES

Use your hands to gently mix the magazine dots into the cotton pulp, evenly distributing the dots. A great way to recycle discarded magazines.

33 Multicolored Dots in Sky Blue Cotton

- 1 CUP SKY BLUE COTTON PULP
- 2 TABLESPOONS (30ML) DOTS PUNCHED FROM PINK, BLUE, YELLOW, AND GREEN TISSUE PAPER

1 Gently mix all the tissue paper dots together.

2 Use your hands to carefully blend the dots into the colored cotton pulp to produce a colorful sheet.

34 Blue Cupids in Yellow Cotton

- 1 CUP DARK YELLOW COTTON PULP
- 2 TABLESPOONS (30ML) CUPID CONFETTI PUNCHED FROM PALE BLUE BOND PAPER

Gently mix the cupid confetti evenly into the colored pulp by hand to create a contrasting paper.

23

Thread and String Accents

Walk through the craft and sewing sections of your favorite store and collect packages of wonderful threads and strings, ranging from natural jute to embroidery floss. Vary the lengths and thickness of the threads, and mix them into a variety of pulps for an endless range of effects.

37

38

39

40

37 Chunky Red Yarn in Abaca

- 1 CUP ABACA PULP
- 1/2 CUP RED ANGORA YARN, RANDOMLY CUT INTO PIECES

Use your hands to mix the yarn evenly into the abaca pulp. Paper will be smooth with large chunks of red yarn.

38 Pastel Violet Abaca Chunk

- 1 CUP PASTEL VIOLET ABACA PULP
- 2 TABLESPOONS (30ML) MULTICOLORED EMBROIDERY THREAD, CUT INTO 1/4 TO 1/2-INCH (7 TO 13-MM) PIECES

Mix the threads evenly into the colored abaca pulp with your hands, to produce a pale purple paper accented with multi-colored pieces of thread.

39 Pale Pink Cotton and Gray Thread

- 1 CUP PINK COTTON PULP
- 2 TABLESPOONS (30ML) PINK AND GRAY EMBROIDERY THREADS, CUT INTO 1/2-INCH (13-MM) PIECES

Use your hands to evenly mix the thread and colored cotton pulp together. Makes a delicate pink paper with gray and pink threads.

40 Peach Abaca with Orange Thread

- 1 CUP PEACH ABACA PULP
- 2 TABLESPOONS (30ML) ORANGE EMBROIDERY THREAD, CUT INTO 1/2-INCH (13-MM) PIECES

Evenly blend the thread into the colored abaca pulp using your hands. Creates a light orange paper with matching orange thread flecks.

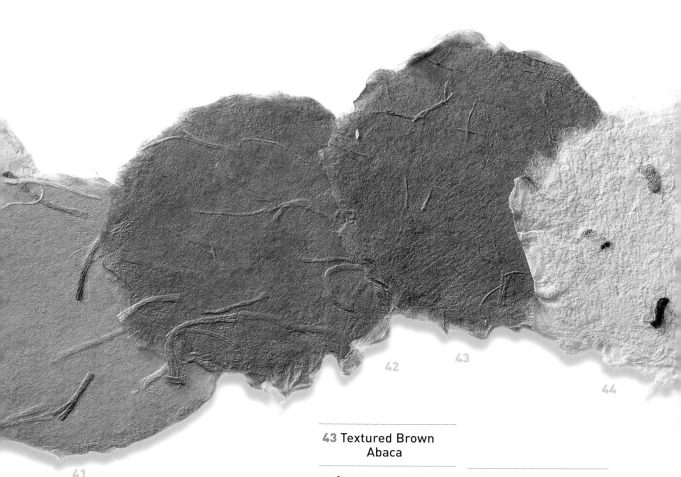

41

42

43

44

41 Multicolored Thread in Tangerine Abaca

- 1 CUP TANGERINE ABACA PULP
- 2 TABLESPOONS (30ML) MULTICOLORED EMBROIDERY THREADS, CUT INTO 1 TO 2-INCH (25 TO 50-MM) PIECES

Mix the thread evenly into the colored pulp with your hands. Dark orange paper will be boldly accented with long pieces of thread.

42 Violet Abaca with Multicolored Thread

- 1 CUP VIOLET ABACA PULP
- 2 TABLESPOONS (30ML) MULTICOLORED EMBROIDERY THREAD, CUT INTO 1 TO 2-INCH (25 TO 50-MM) PIECES

Mix the thread and colored abaca pulp evenly together using your hands. Long pieces of thread will be visible in the violet paper.

43 Textured Brown Abaca

- 1 CUP CHOCOLATE BROWN ABACA PULP
- 2 TABLESPOONS (30ML) BROWN EMBROIDERY THREAD, CUT INTO $1/4$-INCH (7-MM) PIECES

Use your hands to evenly mix together the thread and the colored pulp. Because the thread and pulp are the same color, the paper will be subtly textured, rather than boldly accented.

44 Abaca Flecked with Black Yarn

- 1 CUP ABACA PULP
- $1/2$ CUP LOOSELY PACKAGED BLACK YARN, CUT INTO $1/2$ TO 1-INCH (13 TO 25-MM) PIECES

Mix the yarn and abaca pulp evenly together using your hands. Paper will be smooth with large chunks of black yarn.

Metallic Specks and Sparkles

Collect a whole range of metallic sparkles to bring pizazz to your homemade papers: you need only a small amount to brighten them up. These samples show the results of certain sparkles combined with particular pulp types and colors. You will discover many more combinations as you experiment at home.

47

45

46

45 Gold Sparkle in Cotton

- 1 CUP COTTON PULP
- 2 TABLESPOONS (30ML) GOLD SPARKLES

Blend the sparkles into the cotton pulp by hand to produce a beautiful white paper amply strewn with golden sparkles.

46 Pink Cotton with Iridescent Sparkles

- 1 CUP PINK COTTON PULP
- 2 TABLESPOONS (30ML) WHITE IRIDESCENT SPARKLES

Use your hands to evenly blend the sparkles into the colored cotton pulp. The iridescent sparkles subtly enhance and lend a shimmer to the paper.

47 Gold Sparkles in Blue Cotton

- 1 CUP SKY BLUE COTTON PULP
- 2 TABLESPOONS (30ML) GOLD SPARKLES

Mix together the sparkles and colored cotton pulp with your hands to make an attractive combination of gold sparkles in blue paper.

48 Lime Cotton with Red Sparkles

- 1 CUP LIME COTTON PULP
- 2 TABLESPOONS (30ML) RED SPARKLES

Evenly blend the sparkles into the colored cotton pulp by hand. Lime green paper will be sharply accented with red sparkles.

49 Deep Blue Cotton Sheets with Iridescent Sparkles

- 1 CUP DEEP BLUE COTTON PULP
- 1 TEASPOON (5ML) IRIDESCENT SPARKLES PER SHEET

1 Pull and couch four sheets of blue cotton paper.

2 Sprinkle ¼ teaspoon (1.25ml) of sparkles all over the surface of each sheet before pressing and drying. Creates a very sparkly sheet.

48

49

50 Deep Green Cotton Sheets with Silver Sparkles

- 1 CUP DEEP GREEN COTTON PULP
- 1 TEASPOON (5ML) SILVER SPARKLES PER SHEET

1 Pull and couch four sheets of deep green cotton paper.

2 Sprinkle ¼ teaspoon (1.25ml) of sparkles all over the surface of each sheet before pressing and drying. Produces silvery sheets of green paper.

50

51

51 Yellow Cotton with Blue Sparkles

- 1 CUP DARK YELLOW COTTON PULP
- 2 TABLESPOONS (30ML) BLUE SPARKLES

Evenly mix the sparkles into the colored cotton pulp by hand for a bold yellow paper generously strewn with blue sparkles.

52 Fiery Red Cotton Sheets with Silver Sparkles

- 1 CUP FIERY RED COTTON PULP
- 1 TEASPOON (5ML) SILVER SPARKLES PER SHEET

1 Pull and couch four sheets of fiery red cotton paper.

2 Sprinkle ¼ teaspoon (1.25ml) of sparkles all over the surface of each sheet before pressing and drying.

52

27

Metallic Thread Accents

How can you produce metallic thread when you can't find it in the store? Buy a small piece of shiny fabric and pull apart the threads. Cut them to size and throw them into the pulp. This opens up a huge range of possibilities, especially if you search the bargain bins for sparkly remnants!

53 Abaca with Gold Thread

- 1 CUP ABACA PULP
- 2 YARDS (1.8M) GOLD METALLIC THREAD, CUT INTO 1 TO 2-INCH (25 TO 50-MM) PIECES

Use your hands to mix the gold thread evenly into the abaca pulp to produce an elegant handmade paper.

54 Abaca with Chunky Purple and Silver

- 1 CUP ABACA PULP
- ¼ CUP PURPLE METALLIC WRAPPING RIBBON, CUT INTO ½ TO 1-INCH (13 TO 25-MM) PIECES
- 1 TABLESPOON (15ML) SILVER METALLIC THREAD, CUT INTO 1-INCH (25-MM) PIECES

Evenly mix the metallic threads into the abaca pulp by hand. Makes a paper flecked with large purple pieces and small silver strands.

55 Pale Pink Abaca with Silver Thread

- 1 CUP PALE PINK ABACA PULP
- 2 YARDS (1.8M) SILVER METALLIC THREAD, CUT INTO 1 TO 2-INCH (25 TO 50-MM) PIECES

Mix the metallic thread evenly into the colored abaca pulp using your hands. The longer threads in this recipe create an interesting effect in the pulp.

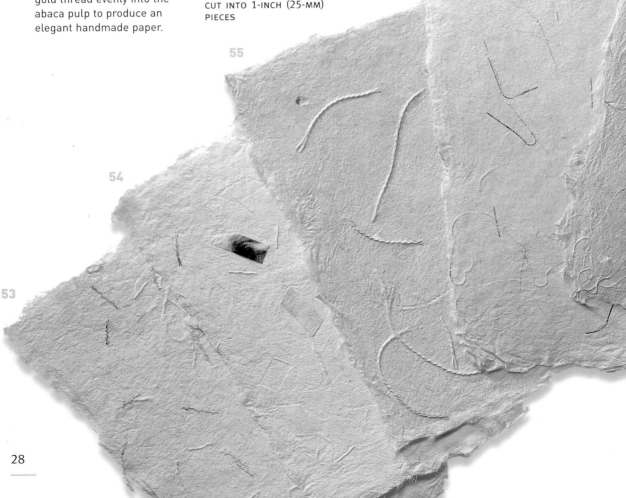

53
54
55
56
57

56 Peach Abaca and Blue Metallic Thread

- 1 CUP PEACH ABACA PULP
- 2 TABLESPOONS (30ML) BLUE METALLIC THREAD, CUT INTO 2 TO 3-INCH (50 TO 80-MM) PIECES

Mix the metallic thread evenly into the colored abaca pulp by hand for a unique contrasting look.

57 Tan Abaca with Silver Thread

- 1 CUP TAN ABACA PULP
- 2 TABLESPOONS (30ML) SILVER THREAD, CUT INTO 2 TO 3-INCH (50 TO 80-MM) PIECES

Evenly mix the silver metallic thread into the colored abaca pulp using your hands. This makes an understated but beautiful combination.

58 Chocolate Brown Abaca and Silver Tinsel

- 1 CUP CHOCOLATE BROWN ABACA PULP
- 2 TABLESPOONS (30ML) SILVER TINSEL, CUT INTO 1 TO 3-INCH (25 TO 80-MM) PIECES

Mix the tinsel evenly into the colored abaca pulp with your hands. This dark brown paper with silver flecks contrasts well with the Tan Abaca with Silver Thread.

59 Tangerine Abaca with Gold Tinsel

- 1 CUP TANGERINE ABACA PULP
- 2 TABLESPOONS (30ML) GOLD TINSEL, CUT INTO 1 TO 3-INCH (25 TO 80-MM) PIECES

Mix the tinsel and colored abaca pulp together evenly by hand. Dark orange paper will be accented with gold tinsel.

60 Violet Abaca and Gold Foil Wrap

- 1 CUP VIOLET ABACA PULP
- $\frac{1}{2}$ CUP GOLD FOIL, RANDOMLY CUT INTO STRIPS

As well as possible, mix the gold foil into the colored abaca pulp with your hands. Foil will appear very boldly in the purple paper.

58

59

60

Sprinklings of Metallic Confetti

Many shapes and sizes of metallic confetti are available to buy, but if you want a custom look, purchase foil wrapping paper and use a hole punch or specialty punches to make your own confetti combinations. This paper is great for making custom greeting cards for special occasions.

61 Moon and Stars in Green Cotton

- 1 CUP LIME GREEN COTTON PULP
- 2 TEASPOONS (10ML) METALLIC MOON AND STAR CONFETTI

Mix the confetti evenly into the colored cotton pulp, using your hands to avoid breaking the shapes. Creates a beautiful green paper accented with shimmering moons and stars.

62 Metallic Confetti Shapes in Sunny Yellow Cotton

- 1 CUP LEMON COTTON PULP
- 2 TEASPOONS (10ML) ASSORTED METALLIC CONFETTI

Gently blend the metallic confetti into the colored cotton pulp using your hands. Make a sunny yellow paper flecked with different confetti shapes.

63 Multicolored Stars in Blue Cotton

- 1 CUP SKY BLUE COTTON PULP
- 2 TEASPOONS (10ML) MULTICOLORED METALLIC STAR CONFETTI

Mix together the multicolored metallic confetti and colored cotton pulp with your hands, aiming for an even distribution of shapes. Makes a star-studded paper.

64 Multicolored Foil Confetti in Pink Cotton

- 1 CUP PINK COTTON PULP
- 2 TABLESPOONS (30ML) MULTICOLORED FOIL CONFETTI

Evenly mix the foil confetti into the colored pulp using your hands. This paper will be liberally strewn with multicolored confetti.

65

66

67

68

65 Gold Foil Confetti in Blue Cotton

- 1 CUP DEEP BLUE COTTON PULP
- 2 TABLESPOONS (30ML) GOLD FOIL CONFETTI

Mix together the gold foil confetti and colored cotton pulp with your hands, aiming for an even distribution of confetti. This paper pairs the classic colors of blue and gold, which never fail to look good together.

66 Aluminum Foil Confetti in Fiery Red Cotton

- 1 CUP FIERY RED COTTON PULP
- 2 TABLESPOONS (30ML) ALUMINUM FOIL, RANDOMLY CUT INTO PIECES

Evenly mix together the aluminum foil and colored cotton pulp with your hands, leaving large silver chunks in the pulp.

67 Gold Heart Confetti in Green Cotton

- 1 CUP DEEP GREEN COTTON PULP
- 3 TEASPOONS (15ML) GOLD HEART CONFETTI

Use your hands to mix the gold confetti evenly into the colored cotton pulp. Paper will be lightly flecked with gold hearts.

68 Iridescent Heart Confetti in Yellow Cotton

- 1 CUP DARK YELLOW COTTON PULP
- 2 TEASPOONS (10ML) IRIDESCENT HEART CONFETTI

Evenly mix together the iridescent confetti and the colored pulp using your hands. Hearts will shimmer in the pulp.

Textured Papers

One of the many intriguing qualities of making your own paper is the potential you have to produce hundreds of textured surfaces. Using everyday items from around the home and in the workshop, you can design amazing wall hangings, matting for artwork or photography, artist's paper, and much more.

Toweling and other textured fabrics will give your paper distinct surfaces, especially if the sheet is couched directly onto the fabric and allowed to air dry under the pressure of a weight. A brick placed on a board will provide a simple weight to emboss a design on a single sheet.

You can choose to make just one textured sheet or several at a time. Remember to drain unused pulp and store it in a labeled, airtight container in the refrigerator.

The following recipes use prepared pulp and pulled sheets. For details on blending pulp and pulling sheets, as well as couching, pressing, and drying, see pages 8 to 13.

Particular pulps are not always specified in this chapter as the techniques described will work on most pulp types—feel free to experiment with cotton, abaca, recycled, and colored pulps.

Textured Paper Samplers

Examine and try out these samples, which use some common methods of giving paper texture, then experiment with other objects in your home and environment to discover new looks and textures for your paper. Remember to record your findings so that you can reproduce particular papers whenever you want.

72

69 Corrugated Cardboard Allover Texture

- 1 CUP PULP
- SHEET OF CORRUGATED CARDBOARD, SLIGHTLY LARGER THAN THE MOLD
- URETHANE-BASED WATERPROOF FIXATIVE, OPTIONAL

1 If you plan to reuse the cardboard sheet, first coat it with a waterproof fixative.

2 Couch a sheet of paper directly onto the corrugated cardboard and leave to air dry.

3 When dry, carefully peel the sheet away from the cardboard to reveal a consistent texture across the paper.

71 Styrofoam-embossed Sheet

- 1 CUP PULP
- SHEET OF STYROFOAM, SLIGHTLY LARGER THAN THE MOLD

1 Scrape the Styrofoam sheets with a paring knife to roughen the surface.

2 Couch a sheet of paper directly onto the Styrofoam.

3 Protect the paper and weigh it down. Allow to air dry.

4 Carefully peel the dry sheet off the Styrofoam to reveal a heavily textured surface.

72 Wire-heart Embossed Motif

- 1 CUP PULP
- MEDIUM-GAUGE CRAFT WIRE

1 Bend a piece of medium-gauge craft wire into the desired shape, here a heart.

2 Couch the sheet of paper onto the shape.

3 Protect the sheet as necessary and weigh it down. Leave to air dry.

4 When completely dry, carefully peel the wire off the paper, leaving the heart shape quite visible.

71

70

70 Brick-embossed Sheet

- 1 CUP PULP
- HOUSE BRICKS

1 Couch a sheet of paper directly onto the bricks.

2 Protect the sheet before applying a weight. Leave to air dry.

3 Peel the dry sheet carefully away from the brick and flatten the edges with a warm iron. Try using bricks with various textures.

69

Texture with Household Objects

Try couching a new sheet onto screen surfaces that might impart an interesting texture—window screens, spatter screens from frying pans, barbecue grills, shoe soles—and allow the paper to air dry under a stabilizing weight.

Woven surfaces are also worth trying as embossing surfaces—bamboo, wicker, and plastic basket weaves all produce different effects. Apply weight when possible; otherwise, press the damp sheet firmly into the pattern and air dry.

73 Coarse Wire-screen-printed Sheet

- 1 CUP PULP
- SHEET OF COARSE WIRE SCREENING, SLIGHTLY LARGER THAN THE MOLD

1 Couch and press a sheet of paper, then position the damp sheet on the screening.

2 Protect the sheet accordingly, before applying a suitable weight. Leave to air dry.

3 When dry, gently peel off the sheet to reveal the screen's pattern on the paper.

74 Embossing with the Outside of a Woven Basket

- 1 CUP PULP
- WOVEN BASKET

1 Couch the new sheet of paper directly over the outside of the basket and leave to air dry.

2 Carefully peel off the dry sheet and flatten the edges with a warm iron. Many woven baskets have lovely patterns which emboss well on handmade paper.

75 Window-screen-printed Sheet

- 1 CUP PULP
- CLEAN, RUST PROOF WINDOW SCREEN, SLIGHTLY LARGER THAN THE MOLD

1 Couch and press a fresh sheet of paper.

2 Lay the damp sheet flat on the screening.

3 Protect the sheet as necessary and weigh it down. Allow to air dry.

4 Gently peel away the dry sheet. A sheet of window screening is great for embossing a large surface area.

73

74

75

76

76 Sheet Embossed with Barbecue Grill

- 1 CUP PULP
- WIRE BARBECUE GRILL

1 Couch a sheet of paper directly onto the wire grill.

2 Cover and apply weight. Leave to dry for 24 hours or longer. Here is an example of what can happen if the screening material is not rust proof! This may be a desired effect, but one way to minimize rusting is to dry the paper with a blow dryer at low speed and temperature.

77 Woven Place Mat-embossed Sheet

- 1 CUP PULP
- WOVEN PLACE MAT, SLIGHTLY LARGER THAN THE MOLD

1 Couch a sheet of paper directly onto the place mat.

2 Cover the sheet, weigh it down, and leave to air dry.

3 Carefully peel off the dry sheet to reveal the pattern all over the sheet. Bleeding may occur, as it has here.

78 Sole Survivor: Shoe-printed Sheet

- 1 CUP PULP
- SHOE WITH INTERESTING SOLE PATTERN

1 Couch a sheet of paper directly onto the sole of the shoe. Weigh the shoe down if possible, and leave the sheet to air dry.

2 Peel away the dry sheet and flatten the edges with a warm iron. If you don't usually think to examine your soles, this sample is good reason to start doing so.

79 Embossing with the Outside of a Plastic Basket

- 1 CUP PULP
- PLASTIC BASKET WITH PRONOUNCED PATTERN

1 Couch a sheet of paper directly onto the outside of the plastic basket.

2 Leave to air dry. The sheet will dry quicker if the basket pattern has a lot of air spaces.

3 Carefully peel the dry sheet away from the basket and flatten the edges with a warm iron. The sheet will reproduce the basket's weave.

80 Embossing with the Inside of a Woven Bowl

- 1 CUP PULP
- WOVEN BOWL

1 Couch a sheet of paper to the inside of a woven bowl.

2 Place another bowl inside the first so that the paper is sandwiched between the two.

3 Leave to air dry for at least 24 hours.

4 Lift out the inside bowl to reveal the pattern on the paper. If the paper is not completely dry, leave it in the bowl to continue air drying. Flatten the sheet with a warm iron.

Fabric Embossing

A variety of fabrics provide a huge range of possibilities when it comes to giving your handmade papers some extra texture. From fun fur to satin and lace doilies there is almost no end to the list of choices. Buy interesting yet inexpensive remnants or raid your closet for wide- and narrow-wale corduroy. An alternative to fabric, but one that produces a similar effect, is bubble wrap, which you will find in most stationery stores.

81 Lace-embossed Sheet

- 1 CUP PULP
- PIECE OF DECORATIVE LACE, SLIGHTLY LARGER THAN THE MOLD

1 Couch a sheet of paper directly onto the piece of lace.

2 Protect the sheet accordingly and weigh it down with a brick or heavy book. Leave to air dry.

3 Peel away the dry sheet to reveal a delicate pattern across the paper.

82 Embossing with Corduroy

- 1 CUP PULP
- PIECE OF MEDIUM-WALE CORDUROY, SLIGHTLY LARGER THAN THE MOLD

1 Couch a fresh sheet of paper directly onto the corduroy.

2 Protect the sheet as necessary and weigh it down. Leave to air dry.

3 Carefully peel away the dry sheet to reveal a consistent pattern. This sample uses a medium-wale corduroy, but all types emboss well.

83 "Tulle" We Meet Again: Embossing with Tulle

- 1 CUP PULP
- PIECE OF TULLE, SLIGHTLY LARGER THAN THE MOLD

1 Couch a sheet of paper directly onto the tulle.

2 Protect the sheet accordingly before weighing it down. Leave to air dry.

3 Gently peel away the dry sheet to reveal a subtly textured surface.

84 Embossing with a Non-colorfast Woven Rug

- 1 CUP PULP
- WOVEN RUG

1 Couch a fresh sheet of paper directly onto the rug.

2 Protect the paper as necessary and leave to air dry until damp, but not completely dry.

3 While the paper is still a little damp, gently peel it away from the rug. Dye is likely to bleed into the paper, which can be very effective.

85 Burlap-embossed Sheet

- 1 CUP PULP
- PIECE OF BURLAP, SLIGHTLY LARGER THAN THE MOLD

1 Couch a sheet of paper directly onto the burlap.

2 Protect the paper as necessary and weigh it down, or press it lightly between two boards, to emboss with an interesting texture. Leave the sheet to air dry.

3 Peel the dry sheet carefully away from the burlap, which will have left its mark on the paper.

86 Printing with Bubble Wrap

- 1 CUP PULP
- SHEET OF BUBBLE WRAP, SLIGHTLY LARGER THAN THE MOLD

1 Couch a sheet of paper directly onto the bubble wrap sheet.

2 Do not weigh down the paper sheet, since this will cause the bubbles to burst. Simply leave the sheet to air dry.

3 Carefully peel the dry sheet away to reveal a honeycomb effect.

87 Embossing with Raised Fabric

- 1 CUP PULP
- PIECE OF FABRIC WITH RAISED STAR PATTERN, SLIGHTLY LARGER THAN THE MOLD

1 Couch a sheet of paper directly onto the raised pattern fabric.

2 Do not weigh down the paper sheet, since this will flatten the fabric pattern

81

somewhat. Simply leave
the sheet to air dry.

3 Gently peel the dry
sheet away from the
fabric to reveal the star
pattern impressed all
over the paper.

82

83

84

88

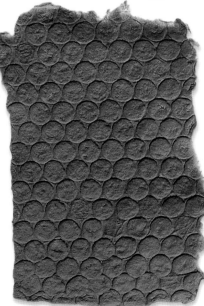

86

87

88 Doily Delight Embossed Sheet

- 1 CUP PULP
- LACE OR COTTON DOILY

1 If the doily is smaller
than the mold, place the
doily on the sheet in the
desired position and couch
a fresh sheet of paper
directly onto the doily.

2 Protect the sheet as
necessary and leave the
sheet to air dry.

3 Peel the dry sheet
carefully away from the
doily for an unusual effect.

Embossing and Layering Effects

To layer different colors or kinds of pulp, begin with a base sheet and couch partial sheets on top while the base sheet is still damp, overlapping in places to reveal layers of color. Or individualize your sheets by couching a sheet of paper on top of a raised shape, such as a coil of jute or a bent wire shape, to create distinctive embossed sheets of paper. Deckles for specific shapes can be made from acetate sheets; to use, place them between the mold and the standard deckle and process the paper as usual.

92 Global Connection

- 1 CUP ABACA PULP
- 1/2 CUP PINK COTTON PULP
- 1/2 CUP BLUE COTTON PULP

89 Waves on Green

- 1 CUP DEEP GREEN COTTON PULP
- 1/2 CUP SKY BLUE COTTON PULP
- 1/2 CUP DEEP BLUE COTTON PULP

1 Couch a base sheet of green cotton paper.

2 Take the blue cotton pulps and use your hands to mold them into wave shapes. Position the wave shapes on the surface of the green sheet, leaving the green visible in places.

3 Protect the sheet as necessary and weigh it down. Leave to air dry.

90 Splash of Orange

- 1 CUP DEEP BLUE COTTON PULP
- 1/2 CUP ORANGE ABACA PULP

1 Couch a base sheet of blue cotton paper.

2 Take the orange abaca pulp straight from the blender, and mold it into various shapes. Position the shapes randomly on the surface of the blue sheet, allowing the blue to show through sporadically.

3 Protect the sheet as necessary and weigh it down. Leave to air dry.

91 Center Square

- 1 CUP DEEP GREEN COTTON PULP
- 1 CUP SKY BLUE COTTON PULP
- 1/2 CUP DEEP BLUE COTTON PULP

1 Couch a base sheet of green cotton paper, followed by a sheet of light blue cotton paper.

2 Use an acetate deckle to couch a dark blue square.

3 Place the blue sheet and square on top of the green base sheet, and continue to process the paper in the usual way.

1 Couch a base sheet of abaca paper.

2 Take pieces of pink and blue cotton pulp, straight from the blender, and use your hands to mold them into different shapes of your own design. Position the shapes randomly on the surface of the abaca sheet, allowing the abaca to show through in places.

3 Protect the sheet as necessary and weigh it down. Leave to air dry. The abaca sheet will be highlighted with splashes of color.

93 Leaf-embossed Sheet

- 1 CUP DARK GREEN COTTON PULP
- INTACT LEAVES

94 Circle of Jute Embossed in Paper

- 1 CUP LIGHT GREEN COTTON PULP
- LENGTH OF JUTE

93

94

95

96

93

1 Couch a sheet of fresh paper.

2 Gently press the leaves into the damp sheet in a position of your choice.

3 Protect the sheet as necessary and weigh it down. Leave for 24 hours to air dry. Remove the weight and make sure the sheet is completely dry before carefully removing the leaf. The leaf imprint will be embossed on the sheet.

94

1 Shape the length of jute into a motif of your choice.

2 Decide where on the sheet you want the motif to be imprinted, then couch a sheet of paper directly onto the motif.

3 Protect the sheet accordingly, then weigh it down to ensure a strong, distinct imprint is produced. Leave to air dry.

4 Carefully peel away the dry sheet to reveal the jute motif imprint embossed on the paper.

95 Common Paper Clip Embossed in Paper

- 1 CUP TANGERINE ABACA PULP
- SEVERAL LARGE PAPER CLIPS

1 Couch a sheet of fresh paper.

2 Gently press the paper clips into the damp sheet to create a pattern of your choice.

3 Protect the sheet as necessary and weigh it down. Leave for 24 hours to air dry.

4 Remove the weight and make sure the sheet is completely dry before carefully removing the paper clips.

96 Dried Orange, Embossed and Layered

- 1 CUP TANGERINE ABACA PULP
- 1/2 CUP DARK YELLOW COTTON PULP
- SLICE OF DRIED ORANGE

1 Couch a circle of yellow pulp, using an acetate deckle, onto the dried orange slice.

2 Protect the circular sheet and weigh it down with a suitably sized book. Leave to air dry.

3 Couch a fresh sheet of tangerine abaca paper.

4 Position the dry yellow circular sheet in the center of the freshly couched tangerine base sheet. Protect the new sheet, weigh it down and air dry.

Texture with String

Placing strings or threads across a freshly couched sheet and then laminating with a second sheet before pressing and drying creates interesting patterns. When the paper is dry, experiment by pulling the ends of the string and tearing the paper to create unusual effects. Combine sheets of different pulp types and colors to reveal a surprise once the top layer is torn.

99 Between the Lines

- 1 CUP FUCHSIA ABACA PULP
- $1/2$ CUP BLUE COTTON PULP
- EMBROIDERY THREADS

1 Couch a base sheet of fuchsia paper.

2 Carefully place the thin threads across the freshly couched paper.

3 Couch a circle of blue paper using a shaped acetate deckle, and press it onto the fuchsia paper and embroidery threads.

4 Press and dry as usual. Creates a unique paper with trailing threads emerging from the circle.

97 Elegant Silver in Abaca Paper

- 1 CUP ABACA PULP
- SEVERAL SILVER EMBROIDERY THREADS, CUT TO DIFFERENT SIZES

1 Couch a base sheet of abaca paper.

2 Position the silver threads on the sheet in a design of your choice. Couch a second, thin sheet of paper on top of the embellished first sheet.

3 Press and dry the sheets as usual. Using a fine silver thread on a neutral abaca background makes for an elegant look. Use your imagination to achieve unusual edges and patterns.

98 Silver Threads in Fuchsia Paper

- 1 CUP FUCHSIA ABACA PULP
- SEVERAL SILVER EMBROIDERY THREADS, CUT TO DIFFERENT LENGTHS

1 Couch a base sheet of fuchsia paper.

2 Position the silver threads all across the sheet in a design of your choice. Couch a second, thin sheet of fuchsia paper on top of the embellished first sheet.

3 Press and dry as usual. A tasseled edge to your paper will set off the delicate texture that appears on both sides of the paper.

100 Checkerboard Squares

- 1 CUP BLUE COTTON PULP
- SEVERAL EMBROIDERY THREADS, CUT TO THE SAME LENGTH AND WIDTH OF THE MOLD

1 Couch a base sheet of blue paper.

97

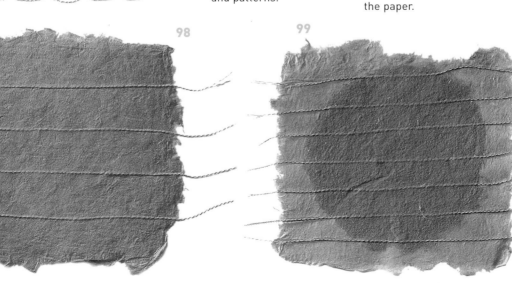

98

99

100

2 Position the threads in both directions to create a checkerboard. Couch a second, thin sheet of paper on top of the embellished first sheet.

3 Press and dry as usual. Different effects can be achieved using different colored pulps and different thicknesses of thread.

101 Jute Sandwiched in Fiery Red Paper

- 1 CUP FIERY RED PULP
- JUTE, CUT TO DIFFERENT LENGTHS

1 Couch a base sheet of fiery red paper.

2 Position the lengths of jute all across the sheet in a design of your choice. Couch a second, thin sheet of paper on top of the embellished first sheet.

3 Press and dry the sheets as usual. Jute provides a more prominent pattern than embroidery threads.

102 Curls in Pink Paper

- 1 CUP PINK ABACA PULP
- EMBROIDERY THREAD, CUT TO DIFFERENT LENGTHS

1 Couch a base sheet of abaca paper.

2 Arrange tiny curls of jute all across the sheet in a design of your choice. Couch a second, thin sheet of paper on top of the embellished first sheet.

3 Press and dry the sheet as normal. Finished sheet will be delicately patterned.

103 Pulled Black String in Layered Paper

- 1 CUP BLUE COTTON PULP
- 1 CUP RED COTTON PULP
- BLACK STRING, CUT TO DIFFERENT LENGTHS

1 Couch a base sheet of red paper.

2 Randomly position the lengths of black string across the sheet. Couch a second, thin sheet of blue paper on top of the embellished first sheet.

3 Press and dry sheets as normal.

4 When the sheet is completely dry, pull back the ends of some threads for an individual effect.

104 Cross My Heart

- 1 CUP ABACA PULP
- $\frac{1}{2}$ CUP BLUE COTTON PULP
- SEVERAL EMBROIDERY THREADS, CUT TO DIFFERENT LENGTHS

1 Couch a base sheet of abaca paper.

2 Position the silver threads across the sheet in a design of your choice.

3 Couch a heart of blue paper using a shaped acetate deckle, and press it onto the abaca paper and embroidery threads. Press and dry as usual. Creates a romantic paper with trailing silver threads.

104

103

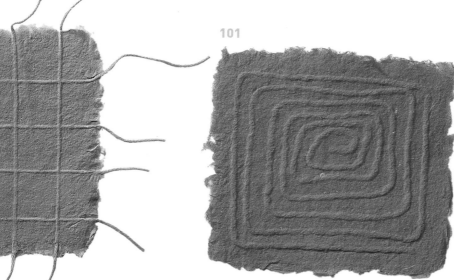

101

102

Pulp Pouring and Embedding

You can "paint" beautiful pictures with pulp. Start with a base sheet and then paint or pour on colored pulp which has been well beaten and thinned with water. Add formation aid to make it easier to work with. Leaves and twigs can also be added to increase interest and texture. Pour pulp into cookie cutters to make unusual or distinct shapes.

105

106

107

108

105 Brown Bear

- BEAR-SHAPED COOKIE CUTTER
- 1 CUP CHOCOLATE BROWN PULP

1 Place the cookie cutter onto a mold.

2 Beat the pulp with water until it is the consistency of cake mix batter.

3 Pour a layer of pulp about ¼-inch (7-mm) thick into the cookie cutter. Leave to air dry.

4 When the pulp is dry, carefully remove the cookie cutter.

106 Blue Heart

- HEART-SHAPED COOKIE CUTTER
- ½ CUP BLUE PULP
- 1 CUP COTTON PULP

1 Couch a sheet of cotton paper.

2 Place the cookie cutter onto a mold.

3 When the blue pulp is the consistency of cake mix batter, pour it into the cookie cutter. While it is still damp, apply the blue heart to the base sheet.

4 Protect and weigh down the sheet, and leave to air dry.

107 Tear Away

- 1 CUP ABACA PULP
- ⅓ CUP EACH OF VARIOUS COLORED PULPS
- SEVERAL EMBROIDERY THREADS, CUT TO DIFFERENT LENGTHS

1 Couch a sheet of abaca paper. Drizzle the watery colored pulps on top, randomly. Place pieces of embroidery thread across the sheet.

2 Couch another sheet of plain abaca paper on top. Press and dry as usual. When dry, pull the ends of the threads to reveal the colors beneath.

108 Pulp Painting: Still Life

- 1 CUP ABACA PULP
- ⅓ CUP EACH OF VARIOUS COLORED PULPS
- FORMATION AID (OPTIONAL)
- SMALL ARTIST'S PAINTBRUSH

1 Couch a sheet of abaca paper.

2 Use the paintbrush to paint on the colored pulps. Try to work quickly, or add formation aid to slow the pulp draining into the base sheet.

3 Protect the sheet and weigh it down. Leave to air dry.

109

110

111

112

109 Pulp Painting: Abstract

- 1 CUP ABACA PULP
- $^{1}/_{3}$ CUP EACH OF VARIOUS COLORED PULPS
- FORMATION AID (OPTIONAL)
- SMALL ARTIST'S PAINTBRUSH

1 Couch a sheet of abaca paper.

2 Use the paintbrush to paint on the colored pulps in an abstract design. Work quickly, or add formation aid to slow the pulp draining into the base sheet.

3 Protect the sheet, weigh it down, and air dry.

110 Scene with Ferns

- 1 CUP COTTON PULP
- $^{1}/_{3}$ CUP EACH OF VARIOUS COLORED PULPS
- SEVERAL FERN FRONDS

1 Couch a sheet of cotton paper.

2 Beat the pulps throughly before using them to randomly decorate the cotton sheet, using a spoon, or a brush for more detail. Position some fern fronds in an arrangement of your choice.

3 Protect the sheet as necessary and weigh it down. Leave to air dry.

111 Take Away #1

- 1 CUP PINK PULP
- 1 CUP BLUE PULP
- $^{1}/_{3}$ CUP YELLOW PULP

1 Begin by pressing small dots of yellow pulp onto the couching pad.

2 Apply a base sheet of pink pulp, scraping away some parts with a tooth-pick, leaving empty spaces.

3 Apply a sheet of blue pulp, which will be revealed when the piece has been pressed and dried.

112 Take Away #2

- 1 CUP RECYCLED PAPER PULP
- $^{1}/_{3}$ CUP EACH OF VARIOUS COLORED PULPS

1 Begin with couching a base of recycled paper and several dots of yellow pigmented cotton.

2 Use a toothpick to remove some pulp before couching other colored sheets on top. Press and dry as usual.

43

Creating Texture by Laminating

Laminate leaves and flowers between carefully couched layers of pulp (line up the corners of the sheets to ensure that they match) and press and dry as for plain sheets. Vary the pulp types, combine colors, and use a variety of ferns and flowers. Try scraping away some pulp over a raised flower to give the impression of it bursting out of the page.

113 Bleeding Hearts in Cotton

- 1 CUP COTTON PULP
- SEVERAL DARK RED PETALS

1 Couch a sheet of cotton paper.

2 Place the petals in a pleasing arrangement across the surface of the sheet. Couch another sheet of cotton paper on top of the first.

3 Press and dry. The petal color will bleed into the cotton sheet for an interesting effect.

114 Petits Fleurs in Abaca

- 1 CUP ABACA PULP
- SEVERAL TINY FLOWER HEADS

1 Couch a sheet of abaca paper.

2 Position the flower heads in a pleasing arrangement across the surface of the sheet. Couch another sheet of abaca on top of the first.

3 Press and dry. The pattern of the flowers takes on an almost ghostly image within the paper.

115 Fern Surprise in Abaca

- 1 CUP ABACA PULP
- SEVERAL TINY PIECES OF FERN

1 Couch a sheet of abaca paper.

2 Sprinkle the tiny fern pieces all over the surface of the sheet. Couch another sheet of abaca on top of the first.

3 Press and dry. Held up to a light source, this sheet reveals the surprising little treasures within.

116 Paper Pull-Away

- 1 CUP ABACA PULP
- CHUNKY FLOWER HEADS

1 Couch a sheet of abaca paper.

2 Place the flower head on the surface of the sheet. Couch another sheet of abaca on top of the first.

3 To keep the three-dimensional look, do not press or weigh the sheet down, simply leave it to air dry.

113

114

115

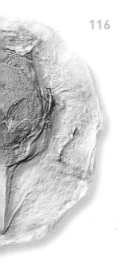

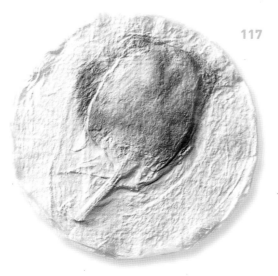

4 When the sheet is dry, carefully scrape away small parts of the paper to expose the flower. Do not remove too much paper however, since the flower may fall out.

117 Raised Flower in Abaca

- 1 CUP ABACA PULP
- CHUNKY FLOWER HEADS

1 Couch a sheet of abaca paper.

2 Place the flower head on the surface of the sheet. Couch another sheet of abaca on top of the first.

3 To keep the three-dimensional look, do not press or weigh the sheet down, simply leave it to air dry. If you prefer a flattened look, press and dry the sheet as usual.

118 Grain in Cotton

- 1 CUP COTTON PULP
- GRASS HEAD

1 Couch a sheet of cotton paper.

2 Place the grass head on the surface of the sheet. Couch another sheet of cotton paper on top of the first.

3 To keep the three-dimensional look, do not press or weigh the sheet down, simply leave it to air dry. If you prefer a flattened look, press and dry the sheet as usual.

119 Secret Message

- 1 CUP OF ABACA PULP
- LENGTHS OF KNITTING YARN

1 Couch a sheet of abaca.

2 Arrange the yarn in the shape of your message.

3 Couch a second sheet of abaca directly on top of the first to laminate the message.

4 Leave to air dry; the message will be subtly discernable.

120 Fine Lines of Silver in Abaca

- 1 CUP ABACA PULP
- SILVER EMBROIDERY THREADS, CUT TO DIFFERENT LENGTHS

1 Couch a sheet of abaca paper.

2 Carefully place silver threads all over the surface of the sheet, overlapping them in places. Couch another sheet of abaca paper on top of the first.

3 Press and dry. Threads can be pulled, when the sheet is dry to make an interesting texture.

Recycled Paper Pulps

Most home papermakers begin by recycling other papers, both as responsible consumers and as artists making use of a convenient and thrifty source of pulp. In this chapter, we illustrate many different recycled paper pulp sources and how they react in combination with other pulps, inclusions, and methods of adding color.

Always rinse recycled paper pulp after blending, to wash away some of the chemicals and print residue that come with any finished paper. Although we have included the use of newspaper and recycled junk mail in this section, we do not recommend these papers as a quality source of pulp, since they contain many chemicals and produce a weak and unattractive paper.

Remember that paper made from recycled products can be difficult to color effectively, since the original paper would have been sized, or finished, with a chemical fixative. To increase the quality of the paper, combine equal parts of recycled paper pulp with cotton or abaca pulp.

For instructions on blending pulps, pulling sheets, couching, pressing, and drying, see pages 8 to 13. Please note that five 8½ x 11-inch (215 x 280-mm) sheets of recycled paper will make approximately 1 cup of pulp. Soak the paper in enough water to cover and allow for some expansion; if necessary, when blending add more water to make the blender operate smoothly. One cup of pulp will reproduce into approximately four 5 x 7-inch (125 x 175-mm) sheets of paper.

Recycled Paper Samplers

Working with recycled paper products is a great way to explore papermaking techniques and allows you to experiment with a wide range of possibilities. Different processing times on recycled paper pulp produces varying results in the end paper. The longer the pulp is blended, the smoother the final paper sheets will be. Experiment with your blender to produce the paper texture of your choice.

121 Smooth Recycled Paper

- RECYCLED PAPER
- WATER

1 Soak the paper in water.

2 Process in the blender for 20 to 30 seconds, using short bursts of power.

3 Rinse pulp to remove ink residue. Paper will be smooth with very light flecks of ink.

122 Medium Recycled Paper

- RECYCLED PAPER
- WATER

1 Soak the paper in water.

2 Process in the blender for 15 seconds, using short bursts of power.

3 Rinse pulp to remove ink residue. Paper will be smooth with some visible letters.

123 Lightly Chunky Recycled Paper

- RECYCLED PAPER
- WATER

1 Soak the paper in water.

2 Process in the blender for 10 seconds, using short bursts of power.

3 Rinse pulp to remove ink residue. Paper will have visible pieces of text.

124 Heavily Chunky Recycled Paper

- RECYCLED PAPER
- WATER

1 Soak the paper in water.

2 Process in the blender for 5 seconds.

3 Rinse pulp to remove ink residue. Paper will be very coarse with large portions of visible text.

Paper from the Home and Office

You will find plenty of recyclable paper, perfect for making pulp, around the home, and many offices and businesses will be only too pleased to provide you with used office paper for your papermaking projects. In both cases, a few things to avoid are: pages loaded with print; staples; Post-it notes; and shredded paper.

127 Wrapping Paper

- 1/2 CUP TORN FLORAL WRAPPING PAPER, IN APPROXIMATELY 3 x 3-INCH (80 x 80-MM) PIECES
- 1/2 CUP TORN COLORED TISSUE PAPER, IN APPROXIMATELY 3 x 3-INCH (80 x 80-CM) PIECES
- 2 CUPS (500ML) WATER

1 Soak the wrapping paper in 1 cup (250ml) of water.

2 Soak the tissue paper in 1 cup (250ml) of water. Leave for 15 to 20 minutes.

3 Blend 1/4 cup of wrapping paper for 30 to 45 seconds, until you have a smooth pulp.

4 Add the remaining wrapping paper and all of the tissue paper. Lightly blend for 2 to 5 seconds, enough to pulp the paper but retain some medium-sized chunks. The chunks will add interest and texture to the paper.

5 Rinse the pulp.

125 Newspaper Pulp

- 1 CUP TORN NEWSPAPER, IN APPROXIMATELY 3 x 3-INCH (80 x 80-MM) PIECES
- 2 CUPS (500ML) WATER

1 Soak the newspaper in the water for 15 to 20 minutes. To reduce the amount of ink in the pulp, drain off the gray water and rinse the newspaper under a tap for 1 minute.

2 Place several pieces in the blender and process for 30 seconds. Repeat the process until all the paper has been blended.

3 Rinse the pulp. The paper will be white with black flecks of ink.

126 Fliers

- 1 CUP TORN FLIERS, IN APPROXIMATELY 2 x 2-INCH (50 x 50-MM) PIECES
- 2 CUPS (500ML) WATER

1 Soak the fliers in the water for 15 to 30 minutes.

2 Process soaked paper and water in the blender for approximately 10 to 15 seconds, until finely chopped.

3 Rinse pulp. Paper will be finely blended with some visible flecks of color, dependent on the coatings on the original fliers.

125

126

127

128

128 Office Paper

- 5 TORN SHEETS OF A VARIETY OF OFFICE PAPER, IN APPROXIMATELY 3 x 3-INCH (80 x 80-MM) PIECES
- 2 CUPS (500ML) WATER

1 Soak all the office paper in the water for 15 to 20 minutes. To reduce the amount of ink in the pulp, drain off gray water and rinse the torn paper under the tap for 1 minute.

2 Place several pieces in the blender and process for 30 seconds. Continue to blend, adding the remaining paper until the pulp is as smooth or as chunky as desired.

3 Rinse the pulp. Blending select pieces lightly will produce a chunky texture.

129 Brown Paper Bags

- 1 CUP TORN BROWN PAPER BAGS, IN APPROXIMATELY 3 x 3-INCH (80 x 80-MM) PIECES
- 2 CUPS (500ML) WATER

1 Soak the paper for 15 to 20 minutes.

2 Place several pieces in the blender and process for 30 seconds.

3 Continue to blend, adding the remaining paper, until the mixture is smooth and creamy. Makes a lovely, light brown pulp.

4 Rinse the pulp.

130 Paper Towels

- 10 TORN PAPER TOWELS, IN APPROXIMATELY 3 x 3-INCH (80 x 80-MM) PIECES
- ½ TORN GREEN PAPER NAPKIN, IN APPROXIMATELY 2 x 2-INCH (50 x 50-MM) PIECES
- WATER

1 Soak the torn paper towels for 5 minutes.

2 Process in the blender until smooth.

3 Soak the torn napkin for 5 minutes in a separate container. Add to the processed paper towels and lightly blend for 2 to 5 seconds, to add color and texture to the white pulp.

4 Rinse the pulp.

131 Telephone Book

- 1 CUP TORN TELEPHONE BOOK PAGES IN APPROXIMATELY 2 x 2-INCH (50 x 50-MM) PIECES
- 2 CUPS (500ML) WATER

1 Soak the torn pages in the water for 15 to 20 minutes. To remove excess ink, drain off gray water and rinse the torn paper under the tap for 1 minute.

2 Blend for 15 seconds or until as chunky or smooth as desired.

132 Greeting Cards

- 1 CUP TORN GREETINGS CARDS IN APPROXIMATELY 3 x 3-INCH (80 x 80-MM) PIECES
- 2 CUPS (500ML) WATER

1 Select greeting cards of different colors to add interest and contrast to the pulp. Soak the torn cards for 30 minutes, longer if the paper is heavily coated.

2 Blend half of the paper for 30 to 60 seconds, or longer to create a smooth pulp.

3 Add the remaining paper and lightly blend to produce chunks of color.

4 Rinse the pulp.

132

131

129

130

Pigmenting—Paper and Paints

Construction paper, the thick craft paper used in schools for art projects, is loaded with pigment and just a few pieces are enough to color a batch of recycled paper pulp.

Adjust the blending times to determine the distribution of color. Long blending times will produce a smooth, even product, while short bursts will result in chunky pieces and separate color within the base pulp.

The addition of a small amount of liquid or powdered tempera (pigment made from egg yolks) will also color the pulp.

133 Dark Gray Paper

- 1 CUP RECYCLED PAPER PULP
- 6 TORN SHEETS BLACK CONSTRUCTION PAPER, IN APPROXIMATELY 1 X 1-INCH (25 X 25-MM) PIECES
- 2 CUPS (500ML) WATER

1 Soak the torn paper in the water for 10 to 15 minutes.

2 Add the paper to the blender containing the recycled paper pulp. Blend the mixture for 5 to 10 seconds to achieve a smooth pulp.

3 Strain the pulp. Some construction paper may remain as flecks; some will smoothly break down to color the recycled paper.

134 Cool Blue Paper

- 1 CUP RECYCLED PAPER PULP
- 4 TORN SHEETS BLUE CONSTRUCTION PAPER, IN APPROXIMATELY 1 X 1-INCH (25 X 25-MM) PIECES
- 2 CUPS (500ML) WATER

1 Soak the paper in the water for 10 to 15 minutes.

2 Add the soaked paper to the blender containing the recycled paper pulp. Blend the mixture for 2 to 5 seconds to achieve a medium-flecked pulp. Paper will be a mottled blue-white. If a more even shade is desired, blend in longer bursts.

135 Yellow Paper with Blue Flecks

- 1 CUP RECYCLED PAPER PULP
- 2 TORN SHEETS YELLOW CONSTRUCTION PAPER, IN APPROXIMATELY 1 X 1-INCH (25 X 25-MM) PIECES

133

134

135

136

- 1 TORN SHEET BLUE CONSTRUCTION PAPER, IN APPROXIMATELY 1 x 1-INCH (25 x 25-MM) PIECES
- 2 CUPS (500ML) WATER

1 Soak the paper in the water for 10 to 15 minutes.

2 Place the soaked paper in the blender with the recycled paper pulp. Lightly blend for 5 seconds. Make sure all the construction paper is pulped, but it should retain some chunky consistency.

137 Baby Pink Paper

- 1 CUP RECYCLED PAPER PULP
- 4 TABLESPOONS (60ML) RED LIQUID TEMPERA PAINT

Mix the paint and pulp together in the blender until a uniform distribution of tempera is achieved. The paper will be pale pink.

139 Pale Yellow Paper

- 1 CUP RECYCLED PAPER PULP
- 4 TABLESPOONS (60ML) YELLOW LIQUID TEMPERA PAINT

Mix the paint and pulp together in the blender until a uniform distribution of tempera is achieved. The paper will be pale yellow.

140 Combo Color

- 1 CUP RECYCLED PAPER PULP
- 1 TABLESPOON (15ML) EACH OF RED, GREEN, AND YELLOW LIQUID TEMPERA PAINT

Blend the paint with the pulp until the particles of color are small but still distinct. For a chunky look, blend for only 3 seconds.

136 Cherry-flecked Paper

- 1 CUP RECYCLED PAPER PULP
- 2 TORN SHEETS RED CONSTRUCTION PAPER, IN APPROXIMATELY 1 x 1-INCH (25 x 25-MM) PIECES
- 1 TORN SHEET BLUE CONSTRUCTION PAPER, IN APPROXIMATELY 1 x 1-INCH (25 x 25-MM) PIECES
- 2 CUPS (500ML) WATER

1 Soak the paper in the water for 10 to 15 minutes.

2 Place the soaked paper in the blender with the recycled paper pulp. Lightly blend for 5 seconds. Make sure all the construction paper is pulped, but it should retain some chunky consistency.

138 Peppermint Green Paper

- 1 CUP RECYCLED PAPER PULP
- 4 TABLESPOONS (60ML) GREEN LIQUID TEMPERA PAINT

Mix the paint and pulp together in the blender until a uniform distribution of tempera is achieved. The paper produced will be pale green.

139

138

137

140

Pigmenting—Tissue and Food Coloring

Tissue paper responds much like construction paper, except that it breaks down even more easily and, therefore, does not require presoaking to break down the fibers, only to extract the dye from the tissue. Try blending fragments of two or more shades and vary the blending times for beautiful results.

Most food colorants are not strong enough to color recycled paper pulp, but they can be dropped onto the pulled paper sheets to produce a kaleidoscope of brilliant shades.

144

142

141

143

141 Pink Pizazz

- $\frac{1}{2}$ CUP RECYCLED PAPER PULP
- 1 CUP SHREDDED FUCHSIA TISSUE PAPER
- 1 CUP (250ML) WATER

1 Soak the tissue paper in water for 5 to 10 minutes.

2 Place the soaked tissue paper and remaining water in the blender with the recycled pulp. Process well for 5 to 10 seconds to achieve a smooth, deep pink pulp.

142 Wasabi Green

- $\frac{1}{2}$ CUP RECYCLED PAPER PULP
- 1 CUP SHREDDED LIME TISSUE PAPER
- 1 CUP (250ML) WATER

1 Soak the tissue paper in water for 5 to 10 minutes.

2 Add the soaked tissue paper and remaining water to the blender with the recycled pulp. Process well for 5 to 10 seconds to achieve a smooth, medium lime-colored pulp. The paper will be a well-tinted shade of green.

143 Purple Chunk

- $\frac{1}{2}$ CUP RECYCLED PAPER PULP
- 1 CUP SHREDDED LIME, YELLOW, BLUE, AND FUCHSIA TISSUE PAPER ($\frac{1}{4}$ CUP OF EACH)
- $1\frac{1}{2}$ (375ML) CUPS WATER

1 Soak each $\frac{1}{4}$ cup of tissue paper in water, in separate containers, for 10 to 15 minutes.

2 Place the remaining water and the recycled paper pulp in the blender.

3 Add the blue and fuchsia pulp and process for 5 to 10 seconds. Ensure the tissue paper has completely broken down.

4 Add the yellow and lime papers, blending lightly to achieve the desired size of chunk.

144 Green Earth Blend

- $\frac{1}{2}$ CUP RECYCLED PAPER PULP
- $\frac{1}{2}$ CUP SHREDDED LIME TISSUE PAPER
- $\frac{1}{2}$ CUP SHREDDED YELLOW TISSUE PAPER
- $\frac{1}{2}$ CUP SHREDDED BLUE TISSUE PAPER
- WATER

1 Soak each color of tissue paper in water, in separate containers, for 10 to 15 minutes.

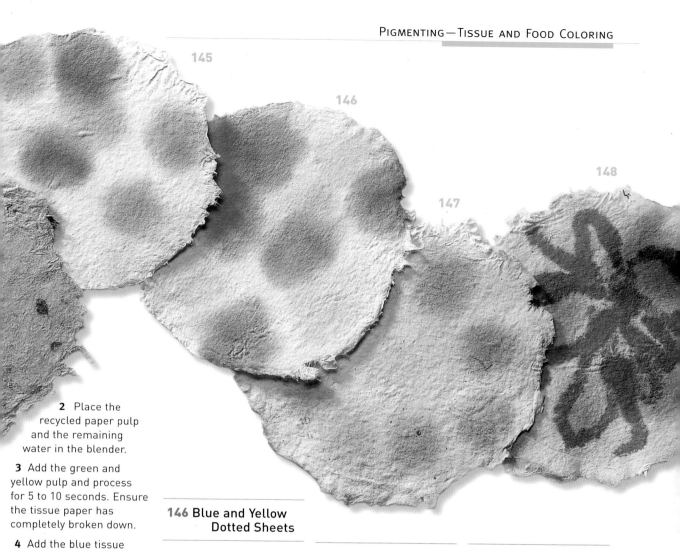

145
146
147
148

2 Place the recycled paper pulp and the remaining water in the blender.

3 Add the green and yellow pulp and process for 5 to 10 seconds. Ensure the tissue paper has completely broken down.

4 Add the blue tissue paper and blend lightly to leave the desired size of chunk.

145 Green and Blue Dotted Sheets

- 1 CUP RECYCLED PAPER PULP
- GREEN FOOD COLORING
- BLUE FOOD COLORING

1 Pull, couch, and press a sheet of recycled paper pulp.

2 Let drops of food coloring fall onto the damp, pressed sheet.

146 Blue and Yellow Dotted Sheets

- 1 CUP RECYCLED PAPER PULP
- YELLOW FOOD COLORING
- BLUE FOOD COLORING

1 Pull, couch, and press a sheet of recycled paper pulp.

2 Let drops of food coloring fall onto the damp, pressed sheet.

3 Overlap dots to create green spots within the joined circles.

147 Green and Yellow Petal Formation Sheets

- 1 CUP RECYCLED PAPER PULP
- GREEN FOOD COLORING
- YELLOW FOOD COLORING

1 Pull, couch, and press a sheet of recycled paper pulp.

2 Let drops of food coloring fall onto the damp, pressed sheet.

3 Pattern the dots to imitate a petal formation.

148 Multicolored Sheets

- 1 CUP RECYCLED PAPER PULP
- FOOD COLORING IN AS MANY COLORS AS DESIRED

1 Pull, couch, and press a sheet of recycled paper pulp.

2 Let drops of food coloring fall onto the damp, pressed sheet.

3 Allow to partially dry, then add additional drops of food coloring. The effect is a "tie-dye" look.

Creative Recycled Mixes

These mixes are the "tossed salads" of papermaking. Here is an opportunity to use up leftover bits of pulp and paper from other projects. To keep leftover pulp, squeeze out the water and store in sealable plastic bags in the freezer. Or, let them air dry into hard "pulp balls" which can be reconstituted at a later date, and store in a box. Warn family members that these are not edible snacks or reserve a section of the freezer just for pulp.

149 Blue Speckled Wrapping Paper

- 1/2 CUP TORN WRAPPING PAPER, IN APPROXIMATELY 2 x 2-INCH (50 x 50-MM) PIECES
- 1 TORN SHEET BLUE CONSTRUCTION PAPER, IN APPROXIMATELY 1 x 1-INCH (25 x 25-MM) PIECES
- 2 CUPS (500ML) WATER

1 Soak the paper in the water for 15 minutes.

2 Transfer to the blender and process for 5–10 seconds to achieve a smooth pulp with light texture. Produces a light blue paper with flecks of wrapping paper.

150 Dark Blue Fleck

- 1 CUP RECYCLED PAPER PULP
- 1 TORN BLUE PAPER NAPKIN, IN APPROXIMATELY 2 x 2-INCH (50 x 50-MM) PIECES
- 1/2 SHEET BLACK CONSTRUCTION PAPER, IN APPROXIMATELY 1 x 1-INCH (25 x 25-MM) PIECES
- WATER

1 Soak the torn napkin and construction paper in the water for 15 minutes.

2 Process the soaked paper with the recycled paper pulp in the blender until as smooth or chunky as desired.

151 Teal Fleck

- 1 CUP RECYCLED PAPER PULP
- 3 TORN TEAL PAPER NAPKINS, IN APPROXIMATELY 2 x 2-INCH (50 x 50-MM) PIECES
- 1 SHEET BLACK CONSTRUCTION PAPER, IN APPROXIMATELY 1 x 1-INCH (25 x 25-MM) PIECES
- WATER

1 Soak the torn napkins and construction paper in the water for 15 minutes.

2 Add the soaked paper to the recycled paper pulp in the blender. Process to achieve desired level of chunkiness of flecks in the teal paper.

152 Peach

- 1 CUP RECYCLED PAPER PULP
- 3 TORN PEACH PAPER NAPKINS, IN APPROXIMATELY 2 x 2-INCH (50 x 50-MM) PIECES
- WATER

1 Soak the torn napkins in the water for 15 minutes.

2 Add the soaked paper to the recycled paper pulp in the blender. Process to achieve desired level of chunkiness. Makes a peach paper with understated white flecks.

152

153

154

149   150   151

153 Turquoise

- 1 CUP RECYCLED PAPER PULP
- 3 TORN TURQUOISE PAPER NAPKINS, IN APPROXIMATELY 2 x 2-INCH (50 x 50-MM) PIECES
- WATER

1 Soak the torn napkins in the water for 15 minutes.

2 Add the soaked paper to the recycled paper pulp in the blender. Process to achieve desired level of chunkiness. Makes a turquoise paper with white and black flecks.

154 Deep Gray

- 1 CUP RECYCLED PAPER PULP
- 2 TORN SHEETS BLACK CONSTRUCTION PAPER, IN APPROXIMATELY 1 x 1-INCH (25 x 25-MM) PIECES
- WATER

1 Soak the torn construction paper in the water for 15 minutes.

2 Add the soaked paper to the recycled paper pulp in the blender. Process to achieve desired level of chunkiness. Makes a deep gray paper with white and black flecks.

155 Lemon

- 1 CUP RECYCLED PAPER PULP
- 2 TORN SHEETS YELLOW CONSTRUCTION PAPER, IN APPROXIMATELY 1 x 1-INCH (25 x 25-MM) PIECES
- WATER

1 Soak the torn construction paper in the water for 15 minutes.

2 Add the soaked paper to the recycled paper pulp in the blender. Process to achieve desired level of chunkiness. Makes a lemony yellow paper with white flecks.

156 Purple Fleck

- 1 CUP RECYCLED PAPER PULP
- 4 TORN SHEETS RED CONSTRUCTION PAPER, IN APPROXIMATELY 1 x 1-INCH (25 x 25-MM) PIECES
- 4 TORN SHEETS BLUE CONSTRUCTION PAPER, IN APPROXIMATELY 1 x 1-INCH (25 x 25-MM) PIECES
- WATER

1 Soak all the paper in the water for 15 minutes.

2 Blend the soaked paper with the recycled paper in the blender to achieve desired level of chunkiness. Makes a purple-blue paper with red flecks.

155   156

Vegetable and Plant Pulps

Although the gathering and preparation of plant materials for vegetable and plant pulp requires some effort and ingenuity, the satisfaction of seeing a handful of mushy brown pulp transformed into a beautiful and fragrant sheet of paper makes it well worthwhile.

Ditches along the roadside house grasses and thistle, which are wonderful pulp sources. Combine the plant material with cotton, abaca, or recycled paper pulp, or use as is. Experiment to see which plants combine best with specific pulp types for the desired effect. Papers made from 100 percent plant pulp, such as grass, iris leaf, or fall leaf, will be somewhat fragile, but can be strengthened with a spray fixative.

Examine the sample photos on the adjoining page which illustrate the effects of straw on different pulp types, and use this information to invent new recipes. Always record your recipes, even if you are not sure you like the look. After drying, some papers take on a surprising freshness and you may wish to reproduce the results.

These recipes use prepared pulps, recipes for which can be found earlier in the book. For instructions on preparing plant materials, blending pulps, pulling sheets, couching, pressing, and drying, see pages 8 to 13.

Plant Pulp Samplers

To prepare straw to add to recycled pulp put 1lb (450gm) of 1-inch (25-mm) pieces of straw into a non-enameled pot. Cover with water and bring to a boil, stirring in 7oz (200gm) of soda ash. Cook for 2 to 3 hours, until the straw pulls apart easily. Drain and rinse twice before combining straw with other base pulp. Cooking the straw in soda ash will ensure that it bonds with other fibers in the base pulp, resulting in a smooth surface ready to receive print.

157 Straw in Cotton

- ½ CUP COTTON PULP
- ¼ CUP PREPARED STRAW

Mix the straw with the cotton pulp in the blender. Produces a crisp white paper with attractive, golden pieces of straw.

159 Straw in Colored Recycled Paper

- ½ CUP GREEN RECYCLED PAPER PULP
- ¼ CUP PREPARED STRAW
- WATER

Add the straw to the green pulp in the blender and mix well, adding water as necessary. Makes a beautiful deep green paper with rich brown straw.

158 Straw in Abaca

- ½ CUP ABACA PULP
- ¼ CUP PREPARED STRAW
- WATER

Add the straw to the abaca pulp in the blender and mix well, adding water as necessary. Paper will be cream-colored with matching straw strands.

160 Straw in Recycled Paper

- ½ CUP RECYCLED PAPER PULP
- ¼ CUP PREPARED STRAW
- WATER

Add the straw to the recycled pulp in the blender and mix well. Add water as necesary. Paper will be white with black ink and golden straw flecks.

157

158

159

160

Celery and Rhubarb Leaves

Rhubarb is one of the earliest spring plants in cool climates and is prized for its tart, pink stems. The large, fibrous leaves are discarded as foodstuff but provide a fine pulp source for the home papermaker.

Celery stalks and leaves can be broken down into a fibrous pulp without much color. Scorch the leaves to add richness and color to the pulp. Prepare celery and rhubarb stalks by cooking with a caustic material that breaks down the fibers and gets rid of the unusable cellulose (see pages 12 to 13). Rhubarb leaves only need cooking in water.

COOKED CELERY

- 1LB (450GM) CHOPPED CELERY STALKS AND LEAVES
- WATER TO COVER
- 5oz (150GM) SODA ASH

1 Cover the celery with water, and bring to a boil.

2 Stir in the soda ash. Cook for about 2 hours.

3 Drain and rinse.

161 Pure Celery

- 1 CUP COOKED CELERY

1 Blend for 3 to 4 seconds, or until the fibers are broken down but still visible.

2 Rinse well, then place in a vat of water to form sheets. This pulp is a little difficult to handle but, with patience, it will make fibrous, light green sheets of paper.

162 Speckled Celery and Recycled Paper

- ½ CUP RECYCLED PAPER PULP
- ½ CUP COOKED CELERY

Add the cooked celery to the recycled paper pulp in the blender. Process well. Makes a moderately textured paper, gently accented with green celery.

163 Heavily Flecked Celery and Cotton

- ½ CUP COTTON PULP
- ½ CUP COOKED CELERY

Add the cooked, drained, and rinsed celery to the cotton pulp in the blender and process for 1 to 2 seconds. Blending for just a short time means that a greater amount of celery remains intact, creating texture and interest.

164 Celery and Abaca

- ½ CUP ABACA PULP
- ½ CUP COOKED CELERY

Add the cooked, drained, and rinsed celery to the abaca pulp in the blender and process well. Paper will be subtly speckled.

161

162

163

168

COOKED RHUBARB LEAVES

- 1LB (450GM) RHUBARB LEAVES, COARSELY CHOPPED
- WATER TO COVER

1 Cook the rhubarb leaves in the water for 1½ to 2 hours.

2 Drain and rinse.

165 Pure Rhubarb Leaf

- 1 CUP COOKED RHUBARB LEAVES

1 Process the cooked leaves in the blender for 5 seconds.

2 Rinse. Makes four fragrant sheets of mottled rhubarb paper.

166 Fine Rhubarb Leaf and Abaca Pulp

- ½ CUP ABACA PULP
- ½ CUP COOKED RHUBARB LEAVES

Transfer the cooked and rinsed rhubarb leaves into the blender with the abaca pulp. Process for 5 to 10 seconds on high speed. Rhubarb pigments pulp very well, lending a deep green-brown color to the mixture.

167 Dense Rhubarb Leaf and Cotton Pulp

- ½ CUP COTTON PULP
- ½ CUP COOKED RHUBARB LEAVES

Transfer the rhubarb leaves to the blender with the cotton pulp. Blend lightly for 2 to 3 seconds on high speed. Light blending leaves visible particles of rhubarb in the pulp.

167

168 Rhubarb Leaf and Recycled Paper

- ½ CUP RECYCLED PAPER PULP
- ½ CUP COOKED RHUBARB LEAVES

Transfer the cooked and rinsed rhubarb leaves into the blender with the recycled paper pulp. Process for 5 to 10 seconds on high speed. The excellent pigmenting properties of rhubarb leaves work very well with recycled paper pulp.

166

164

165

Fibrous Iris and Fall Leaves

An excellent preparation tip when using iris leaves is to scrape both sides of the leaf with the tines of a fork before soaking and cooking with caustic solution. This will make the process of preparing pulp much easier.

The thick stems and veins of fall leaves must be stripped before soaking, or the unattractive, unprocessed remnants will appear in your sheets of paper. These tasks may seem rather tedious, but the end product will delight you and encourage you to try various types of leaves and combinations.

COOKED IRIS LEAVES

- 1LB (450GM) IRIS LEAVES, CHOPPED INTO 2-INCH (50-MM) PIECES
- WATER TO COVER
- 7OZ (200GM) CAUSTIC SOLUTION

1 Cover the chopped leaves with plenty of water, and bring to a boil.

2 Add the caustic solution and cook for about 2 hours.

3 Drain and rinse until the water runs clear.

169 Pure Iris Leaf

- 1 CUP COOKED IRIS LEAVES

1 Transfer the cooked iris leaves to the blender and process in bursts of 2 to 3 seconds, until the leaves are well processed.

2 Rinse. Paper will be golden with delicate strands of iris.

170 Iris Leaf and Recycled Paper

- ¼ CUP RECYCLED PAPER PULP
- ¾ CUP COOKED IRIS LEAVES

Mix the cooked iris leaves with the recycled paper pulp in the blender, processing for 5 to 10 seconds on high speed. The subtle pigmenting properties of iris leaves work well with recycled paper pulp.

171 Large Strand Iris Leaf and Cotton

- ½ CUP COTTON PULP
- ½ CUP COOKED IRIS LEAVES

Mix the cooked iris leaves with the cotton pulp in the blender, lightly processing for 2 to 3 seconds on high speed. Light blending leaves visible strands of iris leaf in the pulp.

172 Fine Strand Iris Leaf and Abaca

- ½ CUP ABACA PULP
- ½ CUP COOKED IRIS LEAVES

Mix the cooked iris leaves with the abaca pulp in the blender, processing for 5 to 10 seconds on high speed. The long blending time means that only fine strands of iris leaf appear in the paper.

169 170 171 172

COOKED FALL LEAVES

- 1 CUP FALL LEAVES, TORN INTO 1-INCH (25-MM) PIECES, STEMS AND LARGE VEINS REMOVED
- 7OZ (200GM) CAUSTIC SOLUTION

1 Cook the torn leaves in caustic solution for 2 hours.

2 Drain and rinse two or three times.

173 Pure Fall Leaf

- 1 CUP COOKED FALL LEAVES

1 Process the cooked fall leaves in the blender in bursts of 2 to 3 seconds, until the leaves are throughly processed.

2 Pull sheets carefully. Finished pieces are fragile and must be handled with care. Paper will be dark brown with visible strands of dark brown leaves.

174 Fall Leaf and Recycled Paper

- ¼ CUP RECYCLED PAPER PULP
- ¾ CUP COOKED FALL LEAVES
- WATER

Mix the cooked, rinsed, and drained fall leaves with the recycled paper pulp and some water in the blender, processing for 5 to 10 seconds on high speed. Combining leaf pulp with other pulp bases strengthens the final sheets and makes them much easier to handle and work with.

175 Fall Leaf and Abaca

- ½ CUP ABACA PULP
- ½ CUP COOKED FALL LEAVES
- WATER

Mix the cooked, rinsed, and drained fall leaves with the recycled paper pulp and water in the blender, processing for 5 to 10 seconds on high speed. This paper will be slightly more deeply pigmented than the cotton and leaf paper.

176 Large Fall Leaf and Cotton

- ½ CUP COTTON PULP
- ½ CUP COOKED FALL LEAVES
- COLORED LIQUID RESERVED AFTER COOKING

1 When cooking the fall leaves, save the colored water from the draining process.

2 Mix the prepared leaves and reserved liquid with the cotton pulp in the blender, lightly processing for 2 to 3 seconds on high speed. The reserved liquid colors the cotton, while the fall leaf pieces add texture and interest.

From the Garden

This section proves that you can use almost any ordinary plant to make great paper. Carrot tops have been rescued from our neighbor's compost and grass clippings from our friend's lawn. Again, cooking is a good idea with these plant materials, but they do break down quite easily and can be cooked without caustic solution (see pages 12 to 13).

COOKED CARROT TOPS

- 1 CUP CARROT TOPS, COARSELY CHOPPED
- WATER

1 Cook the carrot tops in water for 1½ to 2 hours.

2 Drain and rinse.

177 Carrot Tops and Abaca

- ½ CUP ABACA PULP
- ½ CUP CARROT TOPS, COARSELY CHOPPED
- WATER

1 Leave the carrot tops in a plastic bag until they start to decompose, approximately 3 days, before cooking.

2 Remove from bag and rinse well.

3 Cook in water for 1 hour.

4 Drain and rinse.

5 Process lightly with abaca pulp and water in the blender. Abaca pulp is pigmented green and the carrot-top pieces add texture.

178 Pure Carrot Tops

- 1 CUP COOKED CARROT TOPS

1 Transfer the cooked tops to the blender and process for 5 seconds.

2 Rinse. Makes lovely dark green sheets of carrot-top paper.

179 Carrot Tops and Recycled Paper

- 1 CUP RECYCLED PAPER PULP
- ¼ CUP COOKED CARROT TOPS

Process the cooked carrot tops and recycled paper pulp in the blender until well mixed. A flecked paper will result.

180 Carrot Tops and Cotton Paper

- ½ CUP COTTON PULP
- ½ CUP COOKED CARROT TOPS

Process the cooked carrot tops and cotton pulp in the blender until well mixed. Paper will be heavily flecked with carrot tops.

COOKED GRASS

- 1 CUP CUT GRASS
- WATER

1 For maximum texture and a very delicate paper, cook the grass covered in water for 1 hour.

2 Drain and rinse.

181 Pure Grass

- 1 CUP COOKED GRASS

Lightly process the cooked grass in the blender for 2–3 seconds. Produces fragrant sheets of paper.

182 Cotton Flecked with Grass

- 1 CUP COTTON PULP
- $1/4$ CUP COOKED GRASS

In the blender, process the cooked grass with the cotton pulp, distributing the material evenly. Makes a white paper flecked with strands of green.

183 Grass and Abaca

- 1 CUP ABACA PULP
- $1/3$ CUP COOKED GRASS

In the blender, process the cooked grass with the abaca pulp to distribute the material evenly. The brownish paper will have strands of grass throughout.

184 Grass and Recycled Paper

- 1 CUP RECYCLED PAPER PULP
- $1/3$ CUP COOKED GRASS

In the blender, process the cooked grass with the recycled paper pulp to distribute the material evenly. Produces a white paper flecked with recycled ink and strands of green.

Natural Tints and Textures

For centuries, natural pigments from fruit and vegetables have been used to enhance fabrics and papers. These natural colors usually produce subtle shades in pulp and even lighter results in paper. Vegetables like onion and beets, when boiled, produce a concentrated liquid which, when cooled, can be beaten into the pulp to stain it. However, it is the actual onion skins and beets that give natural papers extra texture and interest.

186
187
188
185

COOKED ONION SKIN

- 1 CUP CHOPPED ONION SKIN
- WATER

1 Cover the chopped onion skin with water and boil for 1½ to 2 hours.

2 Drain, reserving the liquid to use as a pigment, and rinse.

185 Pure Onion Skin

- 1 CUP COOKED ONION SKIN

Blend the cooked onion skin, processing lightly for large chunks and heavily for small pieces. Produces a rather difficult pulp to work with.

186 Large Pieces of Onion Skin in Abaca

- ½ CUP ABACA PULP
- ½ CUP COOKED ONION SKIN

Mix the cooked onion skin with abaca pulp in the blender. Paper will contain chunks of onion skin.

187 Recycled Paper Enhanced with Onion Skin

- ½ CUP RECYCLED PAPER PULP
- ½ CUP COOKED ONION SKIN

Mix the cooked onion skin with the recycled paper pulp in the blender. A chunky paper results.

188 Heavy Onion Skin and Cotton

- ½ CUP COTTON PULP
- ½ CUP COOKED ONION SKIN
- 1 CUP (250ML) LIQUID RESERVED AFTER COOKING

Blend together the cooked onion skins, reserved liquid, and cotton pulp for 2 to 5 seconds. Makes a chunky yellow pulp.

189 Cotton Dyed with Onion

- 1 CUP COTTON PULP
- 1 CUP (250ML) LIQUID RESERVED AFTER COOKING

1 Mix together the reserved liquid and cotton pulp in the blender.

2 Allow to sit for 4 to 6 hours, or overnight, to encourage pigmenting. Pulp will be yellow and can be used as is or with cooked onion skin added for texture.

190 Fruity Kiwi

- 1 CUP COTTON PULP
- 5 KIWIS, PEELED

1 Puree the kiwis in the blender.

2 Add the cotton pulp and continue pureeing until well blended. Paper will have green kiwi seeds and light color.

191 Beet Inclusion

- 1 CUP COTTON PULP
- ½ CUP BEET TOPS, CHOPPED INTO 1-INCH (25-MM) PIECES
- WATER

1 Cook the beet tops in water for 2 hours.

2 Drain and rinse.

3 In the blender, process the cooked beet tops well with the cotton pulp. Produces a flecked pulp.

192 Lettuce Inclusion

- ½ CUP COTTON PULP
- ½ CUP CHOPPED, DARK GREEN LETTUCE
- WATER

1 Cook the lettuce in water for 1 hour.

2 Drain and rinse.

3 In the blender, process the cooked lettuce well with the cotton pulp. Produces a pulp with a light green fleck.

65

Tea and Coffee Tints and Textures

Tea and coffee are readily available sources of pigment and pattern. Brewed tea and coffee is used as a dye, while tea leaves or coffee grounds can be added to the pulp to provide texture and shape. Make a very strong brew and try blending in different amounts with various pulp types. The addition of the tea leaves and coffee grounds to the pulp during beating, will roughen the surface of the paper, a finish appreciated by some artists who enjoy working on a "pebbly" surface.

193 Cotton Colored with Tea

- 1 CUP COTTON PULP
- 4 CUPS (1 LITER) BOILING WATER
- 8 TEABAGS

1 Pour the boiling water over the teabags and leave for 30 minutes to brew and cool down.

2 Squeeze the teabags well in the water to extract the strongest possible color.

3 Add the brewed tea to the cotton pulp and mix well in the blender.

4 Leave to stand for 4 to 6 hours, or overnight. The paper will be a warm shade of brown.

194 Colored Cotton with Tea Leaves

- 1 CUP COTTON PULP COLORED WITH TEA
- LEAVES FROM 2 TO 3 TEABAGS

Mix the prepared pulp with the tea leaves in the blender. The leaves add dark flecks to the paper.

195 Wasabi Green with Tea Leaves

- 1 CUP WASABI GREEN ABACA PULP
- LEAVES FROM 2 TEABAGS

In the blender, mix together the green pulp and the tea leaves. Resulting paper is light green with accents of dark brown leaves.

196 Peach Abaca with Tea Leaves

- 1 CUP TANGERINE ABACA PULP
- LEAVES FROM 2 TEABAGS

In the blender, mix together the tangerine abaca pulp and the tea leaves. Resulting paper is peach with accents of dark brown leaves.

197 Cotton Colored with Coffee

- 1 CUP COTTON PULP
- 4 CUPS (1 LITER) BOILING WATER
- 8 TABLESPOONS (120ML) COFFEE GROUNDS

1 Pour the boiling water over the coffee grounds and leave for 30 minutes to brew and cool down.

2 Add the coffee to the cotton pulp in the blender and mix well.

3 Allow to stand for 4 to 6 hours, or overnight. Paper will be light brown in color.

198 Colored Cotton with Coffee Grounds

- 1 CUP COTTON PULP COLORED WITH COFFEE
- 3 TABLESPOONS (45ML) COFFEE GROUNDS

Mix the prepared pulp with the coffee grounds in the blender. Paper will be roughly textured, strong, and durable.

199 Recycled Paper Colored with Coffee

- 1 CUP RECYCLED PAPER PULP
- 2 CUPS (500ML) BOILING WATER
- 4 TABLESPOONS (60ML) COFFEE GROUNDS

1 Pour the boiling water over the coffee grounds and leave for 30 minutes to brew and cool down.

2 In the blender, mix together the brewed coffee and recycled paper pulp.

3 Allow to sit for 4 to 6 hours or overnight.

200 Colored Recycled Paper with Coffee Grounds

- 1 CUP RECYCLED PAPER PULP COLORED WITH COFFEE
- 3 TABLESPOONS (45ML) COFFEE GROUNDS

In the blender, mix the prepared pulp with the coffee grounds to add texture. The paper will have a slightly rough texture and a rich brown appearance.

195

193

198

200

196

194

199

197

Twine Inclusions

From butcher twine to brightly colored string, there are endless ways to incorporate twine into your paper. Cut the twine into long, short, or a combination of sizes. Pull threads apart for a fine, fibrous effect, or use in chunky pieces for interesting textural characteristics. Place carefully or randomly, use many or a few pieces. Just have fun experimenting with a wide array of materials.

201 Fine Strands in Recycled Paper

- 1 CUP RECYCLED PAPER PULP
- ½ CUP RAFFIA, CUT INTO LONG, THIN PIECES

1 Pull the strips of raffia apart to create thin strands.

2 Add to the recycled paper pulp and blend with a wire whisk. Makes a finely textured paper with a lightly flecked background.

202 Chunky Raffia in Cotton

- 1 CUP COTTON PULP
- ½ CUP RAFFIA, CUT INTO 1-INCH (25-MM) PIECES

Blend the raffia pieces with the cotton pulp using a wire whisk. Smaller pieces of raffia create a liberally festooned sheet.

203 Raffia in Cotton with Coffee Grounds

- 1 CUP COTTON PULP
- 4 CUPS (1 LITER) BOILING WATER
- 8 TABLESPOONS (120ML) COFFEE GROUNDS
- ½ CUP RAFFIA, CUT INTO 1-INCH (25-MM) PIECES

1 Pour the boiling water over the coffee grounds and leave for 30 minutes to brew and cool down.

2 Mix the brewed coffee and cotton pulp together in the blender.

3 Leave to infuse for 4 to 6 hours, or overnight.

4 Use a wire whisk to blend in the raffia pieces for a contrasting effect. Produces a lightly textured paper with raffia highlights.

68

204 Raffia Pieces in Abaca

- 1 CUP ABACA PULP
- ½ CUP RAFFIA, CUT INTO 1 TO 2-INCH (25 TO 50-MM) PIECES

Blend the raffia pieces and abaca pulp using a wire whisk. Produces lovely pieces of creamy paper with golden raffia.

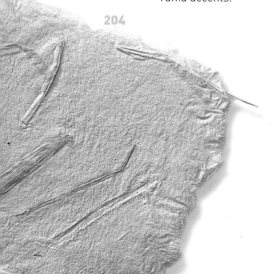

205 Cinnamon and Raffia in Recycled Paper

- 1 CUP RECYCLED PAPER PULP
- 2 TEASPOONS (10ML) CINNAMON POWDER
- ½ CUP RAFFIA, CUT INTO LONG, THIN PIECES

Mix the cinnamon and raffia strips with the recycled paper pulp using a wire whisk. Produces a warm brown pulp with raffia accents.

206 Jute Threads in Cotton

- 1 CUP COTTON PULP
- ½ CUP JUTE, RANDOMLY CUT INTO PIECES

1 Pull apart the jute pieces until you are left with only thin threads.

2 Add the threads to the cotton pulp and mix well with a wire whisk. Paper will be thickly accented with jute threads.

207 Jute Chunks in Cotton

- 1 CUP COTTON PULP
- ¼ CUP JUTE, RANDOMLY CUT INTO PIECES

Mix the jute pieces with the cotton pulp using a wire whisk. Produces a lovely, very chunky paper.

208 Jute Threads in Abaca

- 1 CUP ABACA PULP
- ¼ CUP JUTE, RANDOMLY CUT INTO PIECES

1 Pull apart the jute pieces until you are left with only thin threads.

2 Add the threads to the abaca pulp and mix well with a wire whisk. Paper will be finely accented with jute threads.

Petal, Herb, and Moss Pulps and Papers

Adding petals, herbs, and mosses to paper is one way to extend the summer season and to enjoy the beauty of the garden all year round. Many herb papers retain their fresh scent for several months and all can be revived using essential oils.

Herbs and petals, fresh and dried, can either be mixed into the pulp or sprinkled on top of the couched sheet. Fresh petals and herbs tend to flake off the finished sheet, while dried ones will stay in the pulp, especially if beaten in the blender instead of being stirred in by hand. Try using combinations of fresh and dried petals and herbs, in the pulp and on the sheet, to find your favorite mixes.

There are a few things to bear in mind when working with petals. Do not use petals with green ends, since these will cause yellow blotches to appear in the paper. Rose petals are tricky to work with as their colors are inclined to bleed or change. Spraying rose petals with artist's fixative (follow the manufacturer's instructions) helps them hold their color.

Combine petals, herbs, and mosses to make your own unique mixtures but again and again, remember to record your petal mixes and beating methods so that you can reproduce any paper.

The following recipes demonstrate how to prepare pulp; for instructions on blending and sizing pulps, pulling sheets, couching, pressing, and drying, see pages 8 to 13.

Rose Petal Pulp Samplers

Deep red rose petals cause blue bleeding; yellow and white petals turn brown in the pulp; and pink rose petals become rather colorless. These samples illustrate the effect of fixed rose petals in different pulps. Applying a sizing agent helps to waterproof and seal the paper, which in turn helps to stall bleeding while the pulp is in various stages of formation.

211

209 Red Rose Petals in Cotton

- 1 CUP SIZED COTTON PULP
- ¼ CUP RED ROSE PETALS, CRUSHED TO SMALL PIECES
- SPRAY FIXATIVE

1 Seal the petals with the spray fixative.

2 In the blender, process the petals and the sized cotton pulp for 1 second. Paper will be beautifully studded with petals.

210 Pink Rose Petals in Recycled Paper

- 1 CUP SIZED RECYCLED PAPER PULP
- ¼ CUP PINK ROSE PETALS, CRUSHED TO SMALL PIECES
- SPRAY FIXATIVE

1 Seal the petals with the spray fixative.

2 In the blender, process the petals with the sized recycled paper pulp for 1 second. Avoid overblending which will pulverize the petals into small, unnoticeable pieces. Makes lovely recycled paper with pink petal accents.

211 Yellow Rose Petals in Colored Abaca

- 1 CUP SIZED, DARK BROWN ABACA PULP
- ¼ CUP YELLOW ROSE PETALS, CRUSHED TO SMALL PIECES
- SPRAY FIXATIVE

1 Seal the petals with the spray fixative.

2 In the blender, process the petals with the sized colored abaca pulp for 1 second. This mocha-colored pulp creates interesting effects when paired with yellow petals.

212

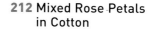

212 Mixed Rose Petals in Cotton

- 1 CUP SIZED COTTON PULP
- ¼ CUP YELLOW AND PINK ROSE PETALS, CRUSHED TO SMALL PIECES
- SPRAY FIXATIVE

1 Seal the petals with the spray fixative.

2 In the blender, process the petals with the sized cotton pulp for 1 second only. White cotton beautifully contrasts with the petals.

209

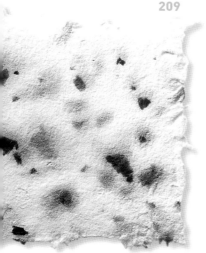

210

Bouquet of Flowers

Handmade papers covered with a sprinkling of colorful petals are sought after and treasured. You can achieve countless variations by mixing assorted petals, following themes such as color, shape, size, or plant family.

Whisking the petals into the pulp when it is in the vat ensures that the petals keep their shape and form in the finished sheets.

213 Summer Petal Mix in Cotton

- 1 CUP COTTON PULP
- $1/2$ CUP MIX OF PURPLE, YELLOW, LIGHT PINK, AND DARK PINK PETALS

1 Mix the petals together.

2 Add the cotton pulp to the vat filled with water.

2 Pour the petals into the vat and blend into the pulp using a wire whisk, ensuring even distribution of material. Makes a beautiful paper evocative of a summer garden.

214 Fall Petal Mix in Recycled Paper

- 1 CUP RECYCLED PAPER PULP
- $1/2$ CUP MIX OF PURPLE AND DARK PINK PETALS

1 Mix the petals together.

2 Add the recycled pulp to the vat filled with water.

3 Pour the petals into the vat and distribute evenly among the pulp by briskly whisking. A natural, recycled paper.

215 Deep Petal Blend in Abaca

- 1 CUP ABACA PULP
- $1/2$ CUP MIX OF DEEP RED CARNATION PETALS AND PURPLE PETALS

1 Mix the petals together.

2 Add the abaca pulp to the vat and water.

3 Pour the petals into the vat and blend into the pulp with a wire whisk, ensuring an even distribution of material. Any deeply pigmented petals are likely to bleed into the pulp.

216 Sunny Yellow Petal Blend in Cotton

- 1 CUP YELLOW COTTON PULP
- $1/2$ CUP MIX OF DEEP RED CARNATION PETALS AND PURPLE STATICE PETALS

1 Mix the petals together.

2 Add the colored cotton pulp to the vat and water.

3 Pour the petals into the vat and whisk throughly, distributing the petals evenly. Creates a sunny yellow paper flecked with petals.

217 Abaca with Orange Dried Marigolds

- 1 CUP ABACA PULP
- $1/4$ CUP DRIED MARIGOLD PETALS, ORANGE WITH DARK RED EDGES

Add the abaca pulp to the vat filled with water. Evenly distribute the marigold petals into the pulp using a wire whisk. The abaca pulp warmly contrasts with the deep orange marigold petals.

218 Marigold Mix in Recycled Paper

- 1 CUP RECYCLED PAPER PULP
- $1/4$ CUP SMALL DRIED MARIGOLD PETALS, YELLOW AND LIGHT ORANGE

1 Transfer the recycled paper pulp to the vat filled with water.

2 Blend and distribute the petals into the pulp using a wire whisk. Using recycled paper pulp minimizes the amount of color bleed from the petals because the original paper would have been sized.

219 Deep Violet Abaca with Dried Marigold Petals

- 1 CUP DEEP VIOLET ABACA PULP
- $1/8$ CUP LARGE, DRIED MARIGOLD PETALS

Add the colored abaca pulp to the vat filled with water. Mix the marigold petals into the pulp using a wire whisk, aiming for an even distribution of material. Yellow petals are a beautiful addition to the vibrant violet pulp.

214

220 Cotton with Yellow Marigold Petals

- 1 CUP COTTON PULP
- $1/8$ CUP DRIED MARIGOLD PETALS, LIGHT TO MEDIUM YELLOW

1 Add the cotton pulp to the vat filled with water.

2 Evenly mix the marigold petals into the pulp using a wire whisk. Yellow marigold petals retain their color well, creating a beautiful yellow-studded paper.

Statice and Daisy

Statice is a hardy flower which keeps it shape even in water. It makes a beautiful partner with other flowers in papermaking.

We discovered in our testing that the magnificent petals of the gerbera daisy turn brown in the papermaker's vat. This is, perhaps, a look that is perfect for certain occasions or uses, but the petals do not retain the fresh, vibrant colors they are renowned for. Other daisy varieties do, however, so you must, once again, experiment with varieties to which you have access, always recording your mixes and results.

221 Purple Profusion in Abaca

- 1 CUP ABACA PULP
- ¼ CUP PURPLE STATICE PETALS AND FLOWER STEMS

1 Transfer the abaca pulp to the vat and water.

2 Mix the petals evenly into the pulp using a wire whisk. Paper will be white with purple accents. Tails of statice flower may bleed yellow, adding additional interest.

222 Light Purple Statice in Recycled Paper

- ½ CUP RECYCLED PAPER PULP
- ⅛ CUP LIGHT PURPLE STATICE PETALS

1 Place recycled paper pulp in the vat filled with water.

2 Add the petals and blend well using a wire whisk to distribute the petals evenly. Light purple statice retains its color accurately, even when dry.

223 Cotton and Yellow Statice

- 1 CUP COTTON PULP
- ¼ CUP YELLOW STATICE PETALS

1 Transfer the cotton pulp to the vat filled with water.

2 Add the petals and blend well using a wire whisk to ensure an even distribution of material. Paper will be white with brilliant yellow accents.

224 Sky Blue Cotton with Yellow Accents

- 1 CUP SKY BLUE COTTON PULP
- ⅛ CUP YELLOW STATICE PETALS

1 Place the colored cotton pulp in the vat filled with water.

2 Add the petals and blend thoroughly with a wire whisk, to ensure a lovely distribution of petals. Paper will be blue with bright yellow flecks of color.

226 Dried Gerbera Daisy in Abaca

- 1 CUP ABACA PULP
- ⅛ CUP DRIED GERBERA DAISY PETALS, DEEP ORANGE

1 Transfer the abaca pulp to the vat filled with water.

2 Evenly mix the dried petals into the pulp using a wire whisk. Dried gerbera daisy petals take on a deep, intense color. Here, the original deep orange has dried to a dark rust color.

227 Cotton Accented with Daisy Petals

- 1 CUP COTTON PULP
- ½ TEASPOON (2.5ML) CHOPPED DAISY PETALS

1 Add the cotton pulp to the vat and water.

2 Blend in the daisy petals using a wire whisk, aiming for an even distribution of petals. Chopping daisy petals into smaller pieces gives the paper more color in smaller dabs.

228 Daisy in Yellow Cotton

- 1 CUP YELLOW COTTON PULP
- 2 TABLESPOONS (30ML) DAISY PETALS

1 Transfer the colored cotton pulp to the vat filled with water.

2 Add the daisy petals and blend evenly using a wire whisk. The daisy petals are likely to turn golden brown in the final product, contrasting nicely with the yellow background.

223

224

228

225 Orange Daisy and Recycled Paper

- 1 CUP RECYCLED PAPER PULP
- ⅛ CUP ORANGE DAISY PETALS

1 Place recycled paper pulp in the vat filled with water.

2 Add the petals to the vat, using a wire whisk to gently mix them evenly into the pulp. Fresh petals have a lesser tendency to bleed and will dry in the paper.

Baby's Breath and Strawflower

The delicate, tiny snowball flowers of baby's breath are a wonderful addition to your handmade papers. They are quite spectacular in deeply pigmented pulp, but make sure the pulp is sized to seal the pigmentation process and prevent the flowers from changing color.

The prickly petals of the strawflower keep their color and shape even after soaking. Their brittleness sometimes causes them to pop out of the finished paper, so we recommend beating them into the pulp in the blender rather than simply stirring them in.

229

229 Baby's Breath with Recycled Paper

- 1 CUP RECYCLED PAPER PULP
- ⅛ CUP BABY'S BREATH BLOOMS

1 Transfer the recycled paper pulp to the vat filled with water.

2 Add the blooms and whisk briskly, blending the blooms into the pulp. Paper will be accented with blooms, which are securely embedded in the pulp.

231

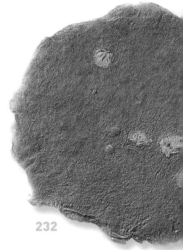

232

230 Cotton and Baby's Breath

- 1 CUP COTTON PULP
- ⅛ CUP BABY'S BREATH BLOOMS

When the cotton pulp is in the vat filled with water, add the baby's breath blooms and blend well using a wire whisk, aiming for an even distribution of blooms. The creamy buds are wonderfully enhanced by the pure white pulp.

231 Abaca with Baby's Breath Blooms and Stems

- 1 CUP ABACA PULP
- ⅛ CUP BABY'S BREATH BLOOMS WITH 1 INCH (25MM) OF STEM ATTACHED

1 Put the abaca pulp in the vat filled with water, then add the blooms and stems.

2 Blend evenly using a wire whisk. The stems enhance the buds in the final paper.

232 Deep Pink Cotton with Baby's Breath

- 1 CUP DEEP PINK COTTON PULP
- ⅛ CUP BABY'S BREATH BLOOMS

1 Transfer the colored cotton pulp to the vat filled with water.

2 Add the blooms and whisk with a wire whisk, blending the blooms evenly into the pulp. The deep pink background is a startling contrast to the baby's breath.

235

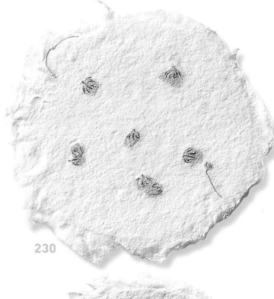

230

236

233

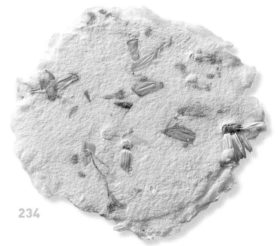

234

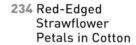

233 Strawflower Petals in Recycled Paper

- 1 CUP RECYCLED PAPER PULP
- ⅛ CUP FRESH OR DRIED MIXED STRAWFLOWER PETALS

1 Mix the petals together.

2 Add the recycled paper pulp to the vat of water.

3 Add the petals and blend evenly with a wire whisk. Strawflowers can be used fresh or dried.

235 Abaca Petal Kaleidoscope

- 1 CUP ABACA PULP
- ½ CUP MIXED STRAWFLOWER PETALS

1 Mix the petals together.

2 Transfer the abaca pulp to the vat filled with water and distribute the petals evenly into the pulp using a wire whisk.

3 Leave to sit for 5 minutes before pulling.

4 A wonderful bleed occurs as the paper is pressed and dried.

234 Red-Edged Strawflower Petals in Cotton

- 1 CUP COTTON PULP
- ⅛ CUP STRAWFLOWER PETALS, YELLOW WITH RED EDGES

1 Transfer the cotton pulp to the vat filled with water.

2 Add the petals and use a wire whisk to distribute them evenly throughout the pulp. This distinctive petal makes a striking paper.

236 Dark Tangerine Abaca with White Strawflower Petals

- 1 CUP DARK TANGERINE ABACA PULP
- ⅛ CUP WHITE STRAWFLOWER PETALS

1 Put the colored abaca pulp in the vat filled with water.

2 Add the white petals and whisk until the petals are evenly distributed. The paper will be tangerine with white petal accents.

Parsley and Paprika

The green of parsley and bright orange of paprika powder are wonderful contrasts and have subtly different looks according to the pulp type used. Try mixing them into the pulp or sprinkling onto a freshly couched sheet for a variety of effects. Use both fresh and dried parsley, chopped or whole, and enjoy the zesty fragrance as you work.

237 Dried Parsley and Recycled Paper

- 1 CUP RECYCLED PAPER PULP
- ¼ CUP DRIED PARSLEY

1 Pour the dried parsley into the blender with the pulp and mix well.

2 Place the pulp in the vat of water and whisk well with a wire whisk. Paper is richly flecked with dried parsley flakes.

238 Fresh Parsley Leaves and Cotton

- 1 CUP COTTON PULP
- ¼ CUP FRESH PARSLEY LEAVES

Add the parsley leaves to the cotton pulp in the blender and mix them together until the leaves are evenly distributed and the size you desire. Makes sheets of paper speckled with beautiful parsley leaves.

243

244

241

242 Heavily Seasoned Abaca

- 1 CUP ABACA PULP
- 2 TABLESPOONS (30ML) GROUND PAPRIKA

1 Mix the paprika and the abaca pulp together in a small bucket.

2 Add to the vat filled with water, blend with a wire whisk. Paper will be darkly flecked with orange paprika.

243 Abaca Sheets Accented with Paprika

- 1 CUP ABACA PULP
- 2 TABLESPOONS (30ML) GROUND PAPRIKA

1 Pull and couch four sheets of abaca paper.

2 Sprinkle the paprika onto the sheets for an intense color. You can create different patterns by sprinkling paprika in or around templates.

240 Fuchsia Abaca Flecked with Dried Parsley

- 1 CUP FUCHSIA ABACA PULP
- 2 TABLESPOONS (30ML) DRIED PARSLEY

1 Lightly mix the dried parsley into the colored abaca pulp in the blender.

2 Transfer the pulp to the vat of water and blend well with a wire whisk. Green flecks against a deep pink background make a delightful, muted contrast.

241 Delicately Seasoned Cotton

- 1 CUP COTTON PULP
- 2 TEASPOONS (10ML) GROUND PAPRIKA

1 Mix the paprika and cotton pulp together in a small bucket.

2 Add to the vat filled with water and blend with a wire whisk. White paper will be delicately flecked with orange paprika.

244 Paprika in Sky Blue Cotton

- 1 CUP SKY BLUE COTTON PULP
- 2 TEASPOONS (10ML) GROUND PAPRIKA

1 Mix the paprika and colored cotton pulp together in a small bucket.

2 Add to the vat filled with water and blend with a wire whisk. Light blue paper will be delicately flecked with orange paprika.

239 Fresh Parsley in Abaca

- 1 CUP ABACA PULP
- ½ CUP FRESH PARSLEY

Mix the parsley with the abaca pulp in the blender until the parsley is evenly distributed. Paper will be accented with parsley.

Saffron and Basil

Saffron is valued all over the world and has long been a cherished source of color in cooking as well as in fabric and paint. Saffron threads are an expensive addition to your homemade paper, but the lovely yellow-orange threads spread their color into the fibers of the pulp in a unique fashion.

Basil is more common in the kitchen and can be used fresh or dried as an additive to your paper.

247 Saffron-infused Cotton

- 1 CUP COTTON PULP
- 1 TABLESPOON (15ML) SAFFRON

1 Lightly mix the saffron and cotton pulp together in the blender, aiming for a lovely distribution of saffron.

2 Add the pulp to the vat filled with water and blend well with a wire whisk. Saffron bleeds yellow, lending the paper a flecked appearance.

245 Cotton Sheets Sprinkled with Saffron

- 1 CUP COTTON PULP
- 4 TABLESPOONS (60ML) SAFFRON

1 Pull and couch four pieces of cotton paper.

2 Sprinkle the saffron onto the sheets for intense color. The red saffron will bleed yellow to create a wonderful warm color around each saffron piece.

246 Abaca Accented with Saffron

- 1 CUP ABACA PULP
- 1 TABLESPOON (15ML) SAFFRON

248

247

246

1 Add the saffron to the abaca pulp in the blender and mix gently to distribute the saffron evenly.

2 Transfer to the vat and water and whisk well. The paper will have a neutral background with flecks and splotches of orange and yellow.

248 Dark Brown Abaca with Saffron Accents

- 1 CUP DARK BROWN ABACA PULP
- 1 TABLESPOON (15ML) SAFFRON

1 Add the saffron to the colored abaca pulp in the blender and mix gently to distribute the saffron evenly.

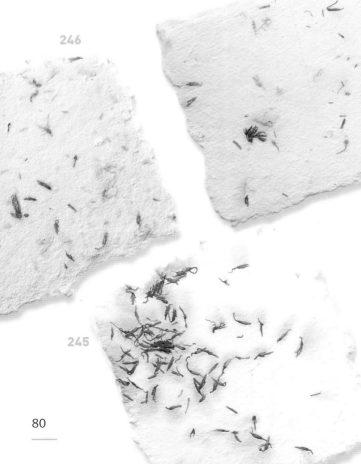

245

2 Transfer to the vat and water and blend well with a wire whisk. The saffron accents the dark brown paper with its deep orange-red tones.

249 Cotton with Basil Buds and Leaves

- 1 CUP COTTON PULP
- 2 TABLESPOONS (30ML) WHOLE BASIL LEAVES, FRESH OR DRIED
- 3 TEASPOONS (15 ML) BASIL FLOWERS AND BUDS, FRESH OR DRIED

250 Basil-flecked Recycled Paper

- 1 CUP RECYCLED PAPER PULP
- 2 TABLESPOONS (30ML) DRIED BASIL LEAVES

1 Add the dried basil to the recycled paper pulp in the blender and mix gently to distribute the material evenly.

2 Transfer to the vat and water and whisk. The recycled paper will be handsomely flecked with dried basil pieces.

251 Sprigs of Basil in Abaca Paper

- 1 CUP ABACA PULP
- SEVERAL SPRIGS OF BASIL, FRESH OR DRIED

1 Pull two sheets of abaca paper.

2 Decoratively position the basil sprigs on the surface of the sheets.

3 Pull two more sheets of abaca paper and couch directly on top of the first sheets and sprigs. Press and dry well. The basil sprigs will be shown in relief in the paper.

252 Tangerine Abaca with Basil

- 1 CUP TANGERINE ABACA PULP
- 2 TABLESPOONS (30ML) DRIED BASIL

1 Add the dried basil to the colored abaca pulp in the blender and process to evenly distribute the material.

2 Transfer to the vat and water and blend again with a wire whisk. Dried basil contrasts nicely with light tangerine paper.

249

250

251

252

1 Add the basil leaves and buds to the cotton pulp in the blender and mix to distribute the material evenly.

2 Transfer to the vat filled with water and mix again with a wire whisk. Basil flowers and buds add color and interest to the basil leaves.

Dill and Turmeric

Here is another green and red-orange combination with its own unique characteristics. The delightful scent of dill and its beautiful, feathery quality make it naturally suited to embedding, sprinkling, or mixing into the pulp. Dry or fresh, it retains its fragrance and, in combination with turmeric papers, makes a lovely set to give as gifts to a keen gardener friend.

253

254

255

253 Abaca Accented with Dill Sprigs

- 1 CUP ABACA PULP
- ¼ CUP FRESH DILL SPRIGS

1 Add the fresh dill sprigs to the abaca pulp in the blender and process gently until the sprigs are evenly distributed but not too finely chopped.

2 Transfer the pulp to vat and water and mix again with a wire whisk. Dill sprigs float within the abaca sheets and add gentle texture and interest.

254 Light Pink Cotton with Dried Dill

- 1 CUP PINK COTTON PULP
- 2 TABLESPOONS (30ML) DRIED DILL

Add the dried dill to the colored cotton pulp in the blender and process to distribute the herbs well. Makes pink sheets that are beautifully flecked with dill.

255 Dried Dill in Recycled Paper

- 1 CUP RECYCLED PAPER PULP
- 2 TABLESPOONS (30ML) DRIED DILL

Add the dried dill to the recycled paper pulp in the blender and process gently to evenly distribute the herbs. Makes an inexpensive, fragrant paper.

256 Large Dill Accents in Cotton

- 1 CUP COTTON PULP
- SEVERAL LARGE DILL SPRIGS

Mix the dill sprigs into the cotton pulp by hand. Produces a paper with wonderful, large dill sprig accents.

257 Turmeric-colored Cotton

- 1 CUP COTTON PULP
- 2 TEASPOONS (10ML) TURMERIC POWDER

1 A little goes a long way with turmeric! Add the turmeric to the cotton pulp in the blender and mix well.

2 Transfer the pulp to the vat filled with water and mix again with a wire whisk. Paper is colored a turmeric-yellow hue.

258 Cotton Sheets Sprinkled with Turmeric

- 1 CUP COTTON PULP
- 4 TABLESPOONS (60ML) TURMERIC POWDER

1 Pull and couch four sheets of cotton paper.

2 Sprinkle the turmeric onto the sheets for an intense orange color. The turmeric adds yellow hues to create a wonderful warm-colored paper.

259 Dark Red Cotton Sheets with Sprinkled Turmeric

- 1 CUP FIERY RED COTTON PULP
- 2 TABLESPOONS (30ML) TURMERIC POWDER

1 Create a striking paper by pulling and couching four sheets of red cotton paper.

2 Sprinkle the turmeric all over the surface of the sheets. Creates a scarlet paper with undertones of rich orange.

260 Intense Yellow Cotton Sheets

- 1 CUP DEEP YELLOW COTTON PULP
- 2 TABLESPOONS (30ML) TURMERIC POWDER

1 Create an intense paper by pulling and couching four sheets of deep yellow cotton paper.

2 Sprinkle the turmeric directly onto the sheets. Produces intense, multi-layered yellow paper.

Thyme and Chili Powder

Cool thyme and hot chili—the perfect combination for someone with a fiery temperament! Try couching sprigs of thyme between two layers of abaca paper or adding a sprinkle of spice for a beautiful, surprising paper, ideal for mounting in a frame or hanging in a window where the light can pass through, revealing the secret inside. Chili powder can be mixed into the pulp or added to the couched sheets. Use thyme and chili individually or in combination with each other or different herbs and spices.

263 Dark Blue Cotton Sheets with Dried Thyme Sprinkle

- 1 CUP BLUE COTTON PULP
- 2 TEASPOONS (10ML) DRIED THYME

1 Pull and couch four sheets of deep blue cotton paper.

2 Sprinkle the dried thyme directly onto the paper. Deep blue sheets are flecked with green.

261

261 Abaca Accented with Thyme Sprigs

- 1 CUP ABACA PULP
- ¼ CUP FRESH THYME SPRIGS

1 Add the thyme sprigs to the abaca pulp in the blender and process until the sprigs are evenly distributed.

2 Add the pulp to the vat and water and gently mix again with a wire whisk. Thyme sprigs float within the abaca sheets and add gentle texture and interest.

263

262 Dried Thyme in Recycled Paper

- 1 CUP RECYCLED PAPER PULP
- 4 TEASPOONS (20ML) DRIED THYME

Add the dried thyme to the recycled paper pulp in the blender and mix well to distribute the herbs evenly. Flecks of thyme will be visible in the final sheets.

264 Fresh Thyme in Cotton

- 1 CUP COTTON PULP
- 2 TABLESPOONS (30ML) FRESH THYME LEAVES

1 Add the fresh thyme leaves to the cotton pulp in the blender and process lightly to distribute the herbs evenly.

2 Transfer the pulp to the vat of water and mix again with a wire whisk. The delicate shape of the thyme leaf appears in the paper.

262

266 Cotton Sheets Decorated with Chili Powder

- 1 CUP COTTON PULP
- ½ TEASPOON (2.5ML) CHILI POWDER

1 Pull four sheets of cotton paper and couch.

2 Decorate the freshly pulled sheets by sprinkling the chili powder all over the surfaces. Plastic templates may be used to create a unique design.

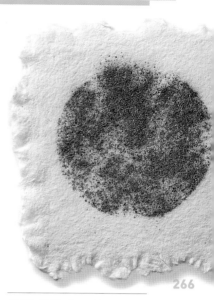

266

265 Abaca Accented with Chili Powder

- 1 CUP ABACA PULP
- 2 TEASPOONS (10ML) CHILI POWDER

1 Add the chili powder to the abaca pulp in the blender and process to distribute the material evenly.

2 Transfer the pulp to the vat filled with water and blend with a wire whisk. The pulp will be strongly colored by the spice.

267

267 Chili Powder in Cotton

- 1 CUP COTTON PULP
- 1 TEASPOON (5ML) CHILI POWDER

1 Add the chili powder to the cotton pulp in the blender and process to distribute the material evenly.

2 Transfer the pulp to the vat filled with water and whisk. Paper will be flecked with chili powder.

264

268 Vibrant Yellow Cotton Sheets

- 1 CUP YELLOW COTTON PULP
- ½ TEASPOON (2.5ML) CHILI POWDER

1 Pull four sheets of colored cotton paper and couch.

2 Sprinkle the freshly pulled sheets with chili powder. Creates vibrant yellow sheets with orange spice accents.

268

Rosemary and Cinnamon

Rosemary is a woody herb with strongly scented leaves. Use it in its many forms—fresh, dried, whole, or crumbled for a vast array of beautiful papers. Cinnamon evokes sentiments of comfort and warmth, and paper can be made with the spice in ground form or in pieces of smashed cinnamon stick. Keep the paper alive with a drop of cinnamon essential oil, or tie a whole stick of cinnamon to a bundle of cinnamon paper with a brown satin ribbon.

270

273

269 Dried Rosemary in Recycled Paper

- 1 CUP RECYCLED PAPER PULP
- 4 TABLESPOONS (60ML) DRIED ROSEMARY

1 Evenly distribute the dried rosemary among the recycled paper pulp using the blender.

2 Transfer the pulp to the vat filled with water and whisk. Rosemary may bleed a little, adding a green tone to the paper.

271 Fresh Rosemary in Cotton

- 1 CUP COTTON PULP
- ¼ CUP FRESH ROSEMARY SPRIGS

1 Pull the rosemary leaves away from each sprig, and add to the cotton pulp in the blender. Process to distribute the herbs evenly.

2 Transfer to the vat and water, and whisk well. This paper makes wonderful note cards.

273 Cotton with Ground Cinnamon

- 1 CUP COTTON PULP
- 1 TABLESPOON (15ML) GROUND CINNAMON

1 Sprinkle the cinnamon over the cotton pulp in

272

270 Fresh Rosemary in Abaca

- 1 CUP ABACA PULP
- ¼ CUP FRESH ROSEMARY SPRIGS, CUT INTO 1 TO 2-INCH (25 TO 50-MM) PIECES

1 Add the fresh rosemary to the abaca pulp in the blender and process to distribute the herb evenly.

2 Transfer to the vat filled with water. Whisk the rosemary into the pulp. Sheets will be strewn with rosemary pieces.

272 Light Green Cotton with Dried Rosemary

- 1 CUP LIGHT GREEN COTTON PULP
- 4 TABLESPOONS (60ML) DRIED ROSEMARY

1 Add the dried rosemary to the colored cotton pulp in the blender and process to distribute the herbs evenly.

2 Transfer to the vat and water and mix again with a wire whisk. Light green paper is intensified by flecks of dried rosemary.

the blender and process to combine the two ingredients evenly.

2 Add the pulp to the vat of water and blend again with a wire whisk. Cinnamon will color the cotton paper, turning it warm brown with flecks of dark brown.

275

274 Cinnamon Chunk

- 1 CUP RECYCLED PAPER PULP
- 10 CINNAMON STICKS, CRUSHED INTO SMALL PIECES WITH A HAMMER

Add the crushed cinnamon to the recycled paper pulp in the blender and process to distribute the spice. The paper will have a three-dimensional relief from the cinnamon stick chunks.

275 Fiery Red Cotton

- 1 CUP FIERY RED COTTON PULP
- 1 TEASPOON (5ML) GROUND CINNAMON
- 2 CINNAMON STICKS, CRUSHED INTO SMALL PIECES WITH A HAMMER

Add the ground cinnamon and crushed sticks to the dark red cotton pulp in the blender, and process gently to evenly distribute the material. The paper will be an intense fiery red with small chunks of cinnamon stick.

276 Light Brown Abaca with Chunky Cinnamon

- 1 CUP LIGHT BROWN ABACA PULP
- 4 CINNAMON STICKS, CRUSHED INTO SMALL PIECES

Add the crushed cinnamon to the colored abaca pulp in the blender and process gently to evenly distribute the spice. Cinnamon sticks add a lovely texture to the light brown paper.

271

274

276

Oregano and Curry Powder

Italy unites with the Orient in this combination of herb and spice. Whole or chopped, dried or fresh, any way is possible with hardy oregano, while curry powder can be blended into the pulp or sprinkled on a freshly couched sheet for very different effects.

2 Add to vat and water and blend with a wire whisk. The green flecks of oregano combine with the print flecks in the pulp for a mottled effect.

277 Sky Blue Cotton with Dried Oregano

- 1 CUP SKY BLUE COTTON PULP
- 2 TABLESPOONS (30ML) DRIED OREGANO

1 Add the dried oregano to the cotton pulp in the blender and process to distribute the herbs.

278 Fresh Oregano Leaves in Cotton

- 1 CUP COTTON PULP
- 4 TABLESPOONS (60ML) FRESH OREGANO LEAVES

Add the oregano leaves to the cotton pulp in the blender and process to distribute the leaves evenly without chopping them

279 Dried Oregano in Recycled Paper

- 1 CUP RECYCLED PAPER PULP
- 2 TABLESPOONS (30ML) DRIED OREGANO

1 Add the dried oregano to the recycled paper pulp in the blender. Process to evenly distribute the material.

280 Abaca Sheets Accented with Oregano Sprigs

- 1 CUP ABACA PULP
- SEVERAL FRESH OREGANO SPRIGS

1 Pull and couch two sheets of abaca paper.

2 Decoratively arrange the oregano sprigs on the sheets.

3 Pull two more sheets of abaca paper and couch

277

278

279

2 Transfer the pulp to the vat filled with water and blend again with a wire whisk. These delicate blue sheets are lightly speckled with gray-green oregano.

too finely. Makes lovely white paper flecked with small green oregano leaves. Oregano blooms may also be used for added color.

282

them directly on top of the first sheets and sprigs. Press and dry well. The oregano sprigs will be shown in relief in the paper.

281 Cotton Spiced with Curry

- 1 CUP COTTON PULP
- 2 TEASPOONS (10ML) CURRY POWDER

1 Add the curry powder to the cotton pulp in the blender and mix well.

2 Transfer the pulp to the vat and water and blend well with a wire whisk. Paper will be tinged yellow with small curry flecks.

282 Cotton Sheets Decorated with Curry Powder

- 1 CUP COTTON PULP
- 1 TEASPOON (5ML) CURRY POWDER

1 Pull and couch four sheets of cotton paper.

2 Place a plastic template with a cutout circle on top of the cotton sheets.

3 Sprinkle the curry powder over the cutout.

4 Pull the template away to reveal a colored circle.

283 Abaca Spiced with Curry Powder

- 1 CUP ABACA PULP
- 2 TEASPOONS (10ML) CURRY POWDER

1 Add the curry powder to the abaca pulp in the blender and process to distribute the material evenly.

2 Transfer to the vat of water and blend well with a wire whisk. The paper will be warmly flecked with orange curry powder.

284 Spiced Cotton Flecked with Tarragon

- 1 CUP COTTON PULP
- 4 TEASPOONS (20ML) CURRY POWDER
- 11 TABLESPOONS (165ML) FRESH TARRAGON LEAVES

1 Add the curry powder to the cotton pulp in the blender and process until the pulp is light yellow in hue.

2 Add the tarragon leaves and lightly mix to distribute the material. Paper will be a strong yellow with flecks of tarragon.

280

281

283

284

Lavender and Moss

One of our favorite papers is a violet-pigmented cotton pulp with little bits of crushed lavender in it. The fragrance lasts a long time, making this paper perfect for drawer liners or a bookmark to scent a special volume of poetry. The addition of moss to paper is unusual but quite lovely and can have very different looks depending on whether dried or fresh moss is used—fresh green moss will bleed yellow in some pulp types, while the dried moss generally retains its color and adds nice texture and variety.

285

286

287

285 Lilac Abaca with Lavender Leaves

- 1 CUP LIGHT LILAC ABACA PULP
- 2 TABLESPOONS (30ML) FRESH LAVENDER LEAVES

Add the fresh lavender leaves to the lilac abaca pulp in the blender and process well, distributing the material evenly. Makes lovely lilac paper flecked with small green lavender leaves. Lavender blooms may also be used for added color.

286 Lavender Buds in Abaca

- 1 CUP ABACA PULP
- 4 TABLESPOONS (60ML) LAVENDER BUDS

1 Add the lavender buds to the abaca pulp in the blender and process lightly to distribute the material.

2 Transfer the pulp to the vat filled with water and blend again with a wire whisk. Makes a lovely creamy-colored paper with a liberal sprinkling of lavender.

287 Cotton with Lavender Buds

- 1 CUP COTTON PULP
- 2 TABLESPOONS (30ML) LAVENDER BUDS

1 Add the lavender buds to the cotton pulp in the blender and process lightly to distribute the material.

2 Transfer the pulp to the vat filled with water and blend again with a wire whisk. Lavender buds may bleed yellow or green, adding interest to the paper.

288 Fuchsia Abaca with Lavender Leaves

- 1 CUP FUCHSIA ABACA PULP
- 2 TABLESPOONS (30ML) LAVENDER LEAVES

1 Add the fresh lavender leaves to the fuchsia abaca pulp in the blender and process well to evenly distribute the material.

2 Transfer the pulp to the vat of water and whisk thoroughly. Use this paper as sachet holders for pot pourri or as drawer liners.

289 Spanish Moss in Cotton

- 1 CUP COTTON PULP
- ½ CUP SPANISH MOSS, CUT INTO 1-INCH (25-MM) PIECES

Add the moss to the cotton pulp in the blender and process well, evenly distributing the material. Spanish moss adds texture to the paper.

290 Spanish Moss and Petals in Cotton

- 1 CUP COTTON PULP
- ½ CUP SPANISH MOSS, CUT INTO 1-INCH (25-MM) PIECES
- 2 TABLESPOONS (30ML) MIXED PETALS

1 Add the moss to the cotton pulp in the blender and process well to evenly distribute the material.

2 Add the petals and gently mix them in. Petals add further interest to moss paper.

291 Fresh Moss in Recycled Paper

- 1 CUP RECYCLED PAPER PULP
- ½ CUP FRESH MOSS, CUT INTO ½-INCH (13-MM) PIECES

Evenly distribute the fresh moss among the recycled paper pulp using the blender. Fresh moss appears feathery and delicate when dry.

292 Fresh Moss and Petals in Recycled Paper

- 1 CUP RECYCLED PAPER PULP
- ½ CUP FRESH MOSS, CUT INTO ½-INCH (13-MM) PIECES
- 4 TABLESPOONS (60ML) MIXED PETALS

1 Add the fresh moss pieces to the recycled paper pulp in the blender and process well to evenly distribute the material.

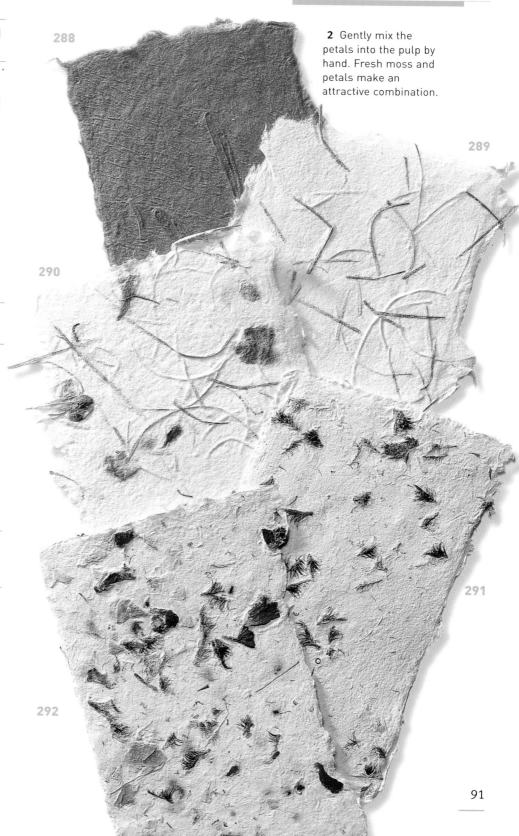

2 Gently mix the petals into the pulp by hand. Fresh moss and petals make an attractive combination.

Mint and Ferns

Mint is one of the best herbs for holding its scent throughout the papermaking process, so it is great for stationery products and gift items. Use as book pages, which will hold the subtle scent of mint for months.

Ferns are one of the most widely used plants in handmade paper, and different varieties often reflect the available greenery of the area the paper was made in.

293 Mint Leaves in Tangerine Abaca

- 1 CUP TANGERINE ABACA PULP
- 2 TEASPOONS (10ML) MINT LEAVES

Add the mint leaves to the colored abaca pulp in the blender and lightly process to evenly distribute the material. This paper has wonderful shades of orange and green.

294 Mint Leaves in Abaca

- 1 CUP ABACA PULP
- 1 TEASPOON (5ML) MINT LEAVES

Process the mint leaves with the abaca pulp in the blender. Creates a creamy colored pulp with delicate flecks of mint.

295 Mint Leaves in Recycled Paper

- 1 CUP RECYCLED PAPER PULP
- 2 TEASPOONS (10ML) MINT LEAVES

Add the mint leaves to the recycled paper pulp in the blender and lightly process to evenly distribute the material. The paper will be liberally sprinkled with mint.

296 Mint Leaves in Blue Cotton

- 1 CUP BLUE COTTON PULP
- 2 TEASPOONS (10ML) MINT LEAVES

Add the mint leaves to the blue cotton pulp in the blender and lightly process to evenly distribute the material. Blue paper and mint leaves together create a striking contrast.

297 Fern in Cotton

- 1 CUP COTTON PULP
- ½ CUP SMALL- AND MEDIUM-SIZED FERNS

Lightly process the ferns with the cotton pulp in the blender. Sheets will have ferns lightly embedded within them.

298 Chopped Fern in Recycled Paper

- 1 CUP RECYCLED PAPER PULP
- 2 TABLESPOONS (30ML) FINELY CHOPPED FERN

Add the chopped fern to the recycled paper pulp in the blender and process to distribute the material. Makes paper lightly accented with fern pieces.

299 Fern and Petal Profusion in Abaca

- 1 CUP ABACA PULP
- 2 TABLESPOONS (30ML) MIXED PETALS, YELLOW, RED, PURPLE
- ½ CUP FERNS, CUT INTO 1 TO 2-INCH (25 TO 50-MM) PIECES

1 Mix together the petals.

2 Add the petals and fern pieces to the abaca pulp in the blender and process lightly to make a colorful paper.

300 Sunny Yellow Cotton with Fern

- 1 CUP YELLOW COTTON PULP
- ½ CUP SMALL- AND MEDIUM-SIZED FERNS

1 Add the ferns to the colored pulp in the blender and process to evenly distribute the material.

2 Transfer to the vat filled with water and whisk. Yellow and green make a cheerful combination.

Resource Directory and Conversion Table

Papermaking Suppliers

Botanical PaperWorks
200–297 Smith Street
Winnipeg, Manitoba
R3C 1L1 Canada
www.botanicalpaperworks.com
tel: 204-956-7393
toll-free number: 1-888-727-3755
fax: 204-956-5397

Carriage House Paper
79 Guernsey Street
Brooklyn
New York 11222
USA
tel: 718-599-PULP
fax: 718-599-7857
orders: 800-669-8781

Lee Scott McDonald
PO Box 264
Charlestown
MA 02129
USA
tel: 617-242-2505
fax: 617-242-8825

Paperwright
1261 Portland Ave
Ottawa, Ontario
K1V 6E8 Canada
tel: 613-731-5417

Twinrocker Papermaking Supplies
P. O. Box 413
Brookston
IN 47923
USA
tel: 765-563-3119
orders: 800-757-TWIN-8946
www.twinrocker.com

Papermaking Journals

Hand Papermaking
PO Box 77027
Washington, DC 20013-7027
USA
www.bookarts.com/handpapermaking

Useful Websites

The Canadian Bookbinders and Book Artists Guild
www.cbbag.ca

International Association of Hand Papermaking and Paper Artists (IAPMA)
www.crafts.dk/org/iapma

Friends of Dard Hunter
www.slis.us.edu/ba/dardo.html

Conversion Table

1 cup = 250ml
1 tablespoon = 15ml
1 teaspoon = 5ml
1lb = 450gm
1oz = 28gm
1 inch = 25mm
1 yard = 0.9m

NB: When referring to pulp the number of cups used in each recipe has not been converted to a metric measure. To ensure consistency, the papermaker is advised to use the same size vessel during the papermaking process as proportion is more relevant than weight or volume.

Index

Credits

The authors would like to thank:
Kelly Burns, papermaker—Kelly worked alongside us making these 300 samples, never complaining about some of the strange things we asked her to do!

All the people at **Botanical PaperWorks** who kept production going while Kelly and Mary produced samples.

Our husbands, **John Reimer-Epp** and **Gary Reimer** who encouraged us to say "Yes!" to this opportunity, and never complained when we spent weekends at the lake with our computers.

Quarto Publishing plc would like to thank **Raphaelle Sadler** for the demonstration of the Basic techniques on pages 9–13.